MAKING
YOUR
DREAMS
∼A∼
REALITY

JEFF WALKER
D.MIN., PSY.D.

CROSSSTAFF
PUBLISHERS, LLC

MAKING YOUR DREAMS A REALITY
Copyright © 2008
Jeff E. Walker

Published by CrossStaff Publishers, LLC
P.O. Box 288
Broken Arrow, Oklahoma
74013-0288
www.CrossStaff.com

Cover & interior: Lookout Design, Inc.

Unless otherwise indicated, scripture quotations are taken from the
King James Version of the Bible.

Scripture quotations marked THE MESSAGE are taken from *The Message*:
New Testament with Psalms and Proverbs, copyright © 1993, 1994, 1995
by Eugene H. Peterson, published by NavPress, P.O. Box 35001,
Colorado Springs, Colorado 80935. Used by permission.

ISBN 10: 0-9800755-0-5
ISBN 13: 978-0-9800755-0-2

THIS BOOK IS DEDICATED TO MY WIFE,

MELISSA

WHO HAS CHOSEN TO JOURNEY THROUGH LIFE
WITH ME . . . THROUGH THE TOUGH TIMES AS
WELL AS THE GOOD. IT IS A JOY TO WATCH GOD
MAKE OUR DREAMS A REALITY
AS WE "WALK HAND IN HAND, SIDE BY SIDE,
FULL OF PEACE AND POWER, REACHING OUT
TO MINISTER TO A HURTING WORLD."

IT IS ALSO DEDICATED TO OUR THREE BEAUTIFUL
AND WONDERFUL CHILDREN,

REBEKAH, AMEN AND CALEB

WHO ARE BEGINNING TO LAUNCH OUT INTO
THEIR ADULT LIVES. MAY YOUR DREAMS BECOME
A REALITY AND BE FULFILLING AND JOYFUL.

I LOVE THE FOUR OF YOU WITH ALL OF
MY HEART.

What an awesomely important and timely book. As I examined this interesting work chapter by chapter, I realized several truths. Not only is the unfolding story biblically sound, it is also lovingly instructive. I have known the author, Dr. Jeff Walker, for more than twenty years. During this period of time, I have observed him following his God-given dream. Dr. Walker writes from years of experience in following after our Heavenly Father in the development of his dream.

In addition to being Bible-based, the book is also a biography of the dream of Dr. and Mrs. Walker. Our generation finds itself plagued by confusion, disappointment, and a lack of absolutes, with the majority attempting to live out dreams originating without any thought of a divine foundation. Thank God for Dr. Jeff Walker's, *Making Your Dreams a Reality*.

HILTON SUTTON, TH.D.

Jeff is speaking to people where they live and about life giving them real purpose, real hope, and real understanding about their dreams. It is a complete "nothing left to be said" book that gives the reader understanding and comprehension. It is easy to apply and live out. It challenges us to say, "Yes, I will do." All there is to do now is let Jeff stir up the dream God has placed inside of you. Get ready to dream!

DIEGO MESA
Senior Pastor
Abundant Living Family Church

Pastor Jeff Walker combines the vision of a dreamer with the heart of a pastor, and he has walked the path to victory, overcoming the joys, sorrows, and challenges of a life of ministry. Through parable and example Pastor Jeff, a family man and servant/shepherd of a growing flock, brings us many gifts in *Making Your Dreams a Reality*.

DR. ALVEDA C. KING
Founder of King for America and
Niece of Dr. Martin Luther King, Jr.

In *Making Your Dreams a Reality* Jeff Walker delivers a powerful and poignant faith-filled message, compelling us to take the leap of faith and, with God's grace and guidance, pursue our dreams, confront the obstacles that block us, and in doing so reach our potential. If you are serious about pursuing your vision, this is a must read.

MICHAEL NEATHERTON
Executive Vice President/COO
Betty Ford Center

Many books have been written on living out your dreams, but Jeff Walker's inspiring, fun, and insightful ways of writing, take it from pie-in-the-sky whims to something tangible and attainable.

BETH JONES
Author of "Getting a Grip on the Basics"

ACKNOWLEDGEMENTS

I would like to acknowledge the following people for their support and encouragement in ensuring *Making Your Dreams a Reality* was completed.

First, I wish to honor and thank Rev. Dr. Hosea Brown, M.D., who first suggested I write this book based on a series of sermons I preached by the same title. Additionally, his financial support helped make this dream a reality.

Second, I want to appreciate those behind the scenes who kept this project on the radar and moved it forward by their invaluable contributions. Many thanks to Rev. Deci Connelly, who continually pushed me along. Her communication with our consultants, publisher, printer, and the like, was timely. Her passion for publishing the Gospel is provoking. Without her commitment, this book would not be.

I extend a special thank-you to David Thomas, Ph.D. Dr. Thomas is a great Bible scholar with a heart that is attuned to the Holy Spirit, and he has been instrumental in the shaping and editing of this volume.

Thanks to Lori McFadden for her help in proofreading and editing. Her appreciation for the written word inspires me, and her assistance was significant.

I am grateful for the practical, "rubber meets the road" encouragement and guidance of Van Crouch and Pat Judd. These men are friends in the truest sense.

The love of my parents, John and Jude Walker, and of my sister, Jackie Walker, serves as inspiration in all I do, including the writing of this book.

Finally, I want to express my deep love and gratitude to all those members of my congregation, who shared words of encouragement and supported me in so many ways. They too are part of the team that made the completion of this book possible.

FOREWORD

BY ORAL ROBERTS

When Evelyn and I had a home in the desert, Victory Christian Center was our church. Jeff and I walked by faith on what is now his church and school campus when there was nothing there but sand dunes and a whole lot of faith. Starting with little more than a big plan, Jeff has made his dream a reality and he continues to do so. He has served on the Charismatic Bible Ministries board for the past 23 years, our youngest trustee ever. Graduating with my son Richard, he also completed his Doctor of Ministry degree at Oral Roberts University...another of his dreams fulfilled.

Jeff has been a true son in the Lord to me, and for the past several years he has invited pastors and ministers to come to my home. Each month different men and women of God Jeff brings gather in my living room for personal ministry. My time with them in counseling, prayer, and impartation is one way Jeff helps other ministers reach their dreams. These servants of the Lord leave encouraged and refreshed, and they experience firsthand Jeff's passion to enrich the lives of others.

Jeff has been a blessing to Evelyn and me and continues to bless the Body of Christ in so many ways. He is a lifelong learner and is a true "original," who is not on a quest to be like any other man. I believe he is an inspiration to others to "press toward the mark of the prize of the high calling of God in Christ."

I invite you to take from Jeff's book the thoughts and ideas that will cause expectancy to rise in your mind and heart, just as if Jesus Himself were talking to you, and to allow God to move so mightily on you that you will not only grasp His dream for your life, but also you will make that dream a reality for His honor and glory.

In Jesus' name

Oral Roberts

4/3/06

A CHALLENGE TO DREAM BIG

"YOU SHOULD GO TO PALM SPRINGS and start a church!" Those words spoken in jest by my friend would serve as God's fulcrum to wrench me from small thinking, little ideas, safe goals, and dwarfed dreams. Those ten words would launch me onto a path which, though thrilling me to the core of my being, would bring out every self-doubt, increase awareness of my insecurities, magnify my weaknesses, and highlight my shortcomings.

Simultaneously, those words would anchor my mind and infuse my soul to such a powerful extent that I could face every challenge and impending danger with courage and faith. Those words birthed a dream in my spirit, and that dream has empowered nearly thirty years of ministry. The reality of that dream has brought success, victory, breakthrough, and blessing to me, to my community, and to thousands of men and women around the globe.

It all began when my fellow Bible college graduate, Joe Bergeron, invited me to preach at his church in Burbank, California. I journeyed from my hometown of Mattoon, Illinois, winding my way through the cornfields and soybeans that grew in the land of my birth into unexplored parts of our country.

Just before reaching my destination, while driving on Interstate 10, I passed through the Coachella Valley in the Mojave Desert and saw the freeway sign, "Palm Springs Next Exit." *I have heard of Palm Springs*, I thought to myself. *I wonder what's out there.* Too weary to stop, I drove the final hundred miles to Burbank and connected with my friend, Joe.

One evening after service, Joe and I were having dinner. I asked him, "What is Palm Springs all about? I drove past it the other evening, and I have seen things on television about it, but tell me what you know about the area."

That's when Joe swallowed his bite of homemade taco, looked across the table at me, and blurted out his humorous retort, "You should go to Palm Springs and start a church." We both laughed. I had never even been there and didn't know a soul who lived there. What a ridiculous thought! But in the ensuing weeks God profoundly solidified that idea in me.

Little did Joe Bergeron know that his words would so lodge in my heart that a life dream would result.

The question became, how could a single, twenty-two-year-old kid, who was raised in an Illinois cornfield and only had a hundred bucks and a beat up Toyota, start a church in a city he had never even visited...where he knew no one? How? By the power of a dream, that's how.

I went back home, and just ten weeks later I loaded all my worldly possessions in the back of my sad little car, stuck the hundred dollars in my pocket, and with the Midwestern crops in my rear view mirror for good this time, off I went...dream intact. Upon hearing the words, "You should go to Palm Springs and start a church," I was on my way to do just that. The road ahead was to be lined with miracles, and the journey was to be filled with both joy and difficulty. I was to learn how God has an exciting experience for any man or woman who will dare to allow themselves to dream.

This book is meant to be a challenge. It is a challenge to you and it is a challenge to me. I write it because I want to challenge us both to dream big dreams, to allow God to stir in us everything He wants to stir, and to move forward in those dreams. After all, God has been faithful in the past. He's seen us through heartache and victory. We appreciate what He has done for us and through us. But we can't live back there! We can't live in the past, whether it was good or bad. We need to shake ourselves and say,

"This is today, and I'm going to live today." That attitude is what will make our dreams a reality.

In the book of Genesis we find the story of Joseph, one of the twelve sons of the Old Testament patriarch Jacob. In Genesis 37 the Bible tells us God gave Joseph a dream. This dream was an encounter with the Lord for Joseph. He went to sleep, had a dream, and woke up understanding the meaning of that dream. Joseph was a supernatural dreamer, gifted by God to understand dreams.

You don't have to have dreams like Joseph had to learn the many lessons from Joseph's life. While you may not have a supernatural dream in the nighttime, wake up, and know the meaning of it; you can still have a dream that the Holy Spirit works in your heart and mind over time. Philippians 2:13 says, **For it is God which worketh in you both to will and to do of his good pleasure.**

As New Testament believers we believe the Holy Spirit works in us, developing in us a sense of purpose, a calling, hopes, aspirations, and dreams. We may not have a physical, literal dream, but we can still have a dream—a purpose in life. The reason I am writing this book is because I want you to have a dream you are excited about, a dream you can invest yourself in, a dream you can move forward into, and a dream that just won't let go of you.

We can learn about this kind of dreaming from the number one dreamer in the Bible, Joseph. His story is found in Genesis, chapters 30-50. In Genesis 37 Joseph was seventeen years old when his father Jacob gave him a coat of many colors. In Genesis 37:4 it says, **And when his brethren saw that their father loved him more than all of his brethren, they hated him, and could not speak peaceably unto him.** Joseph was his dad's favorite. Jacob loved Joseph more than all of his other kids. Those kids knew it, and Joseph knew it too. So we have a little dysfunction going on in Jacob's family.

I'm pointing this out because you might say, "Well, I didn't come from a perfect family. You have no idea what a mess I came from. How can God use me?" Welcome to the club of dreamers who came from not-so-perfect backgrounds! I have got some really good news for you. Joseph's situation shows us that even if you come from a dysfunctional family, you can still have a dream God will bring to pass.

Joseph was in a volatile family situation. His father loved him better than his brothers, gave him gifts, favored him, and exalted him until his brothers couldn't say a kind word to him. In the middle of all this God gave Joseph a dream. The symbolism of the dream was obvious—all his brothers and even his father and mother would bow down in subservience to him.

Joseph's dream was so vivid, vital, and real—and he was so excited about it—that he felt he just had to tell his whole family all about it. He had to say, "Hey, you guys are all going to serve me one day. Isn't that great?" As if things weren't bad enough between him and his brothers! If they couldn't say a kind word to him before, now they hated his guts.

Joseph's decision to tell his brothers about his dream kicked off a long and eventful journey for him. His brothers said, "Let's kill him," but one of them, Reuben, got convicted about that and convinced his brothers to throw Joseph in a pit instead. Then another brother, Judah, came up with the idea to sell Joseph to slave traders who were going to Egypt. Then the brothers could at least make some money off of him.

The brothers sold Joseph to the slave traders. They sold Joseph as a slave to Potiphar, who was one of Pharaoh's officials. The Bible tells us that Potiphar's wife was attracted to Joseph, and she tried to seduce him. But he wouldn't hear of it and began to leave. In anger she ripped off part of his clothing as he ran out the door. To cover her wounded pride and get revenge, she falsely accused Joseph of trying to rape her. That accusation led to Joseph being thrown in prison for many years, suffering hopes born and disappointed. Ultimately, however, Joseph saw God bring his dream to pass.

What I particularly want you to see in this passage is Genesis 37:2, **Joseph, being seventeen years old**, and then in verse 5, **Joseph dreamed a dream.** Now compare these verses of Scripture with Genesis 41:44, where we witness the moment Pharaoh exalts Joseph and makes him prime minister of all of Egypt, number two in the land. Pharaoh said to Joseph, **I am Pharaoh, and without thee shall no man lift up his hand or foot in all the land of Egypt.**

Pharaoh dressed Joseph in finery, gave him his signet ring, provided him a chariot to ride in, and commanded everyone to bow before him. Joseph's dream was coming true. How long did it take? Verse 46 tells us, **And Joseph was thirty years old when he stood before Pharaoh king of Egypt. And Joseph went out from the presence of Pharaoh, and went throughout all the land of Egypt.**

Joseph was seventeen when he received his dream, and he was thirty when that dream began to become reality in his life—a journey of thirteen years. Those were years filled with disappointment and disillusionment, but Joseph's dream was so powerful and life-changing that it kept him going. He never lost faith that one day he would see his dream come true.

In John 12 Jesus used wheat to illustrate what a successful life is really all about. Imagine one stalk of wheat in a wheat field, and on the head of that stock of wheat are all those little kernels of grain. Jesus said, **Verily, verily, I say unto you, except a corn of wheat fall into the ground and die, it abideth alone: but if it die, it bringeth forth** much fruit. **He that loveth his life shall lose it; and he that hateth his life in this world shall keep it unto life eternal** (John 12:24-25). The challenge of this passage is that we not hold onto our lives but lose them in Jesus. Then we will discover who we are and what our purpose is.

Let me encourage you to let God do in you and through you all He wants to do. Don't settle for the status quo; don't love your life just the way it is. It is true the Bible says, **And having food and raiment let us be therewith content** (1 Timothy 6:8). We are not to be unhappy or discontented. But at the same time we are to hunger for more of God—His power, His presence, His grace, His purpose, His plan, and His blessings.

Philippians 3:13-14 says, **Brethren, I count not myself to have apprehended: but this one thing I do, forgetting those things which are behind, and reaching forth unto those things which are before, I press toward the mark for the prize of the high calling of God in Christ Jesus.**

Now here are my questions for you: What are you dreaming? What are you pressing into? What are you moving forward with? How are you challenging yourself in God? Finding the answers to these questions is the point of this book.

We are going to explore a number of things that make us successful dreamers, but before we go any further I would like to give you a synopsis of the basic principles for making your dreams a reality that we will cover in the following chapters.

In Chapter 2 we will be talking about the power that a God-given dream has to transform and direct your life. There are few things more powerful than a dream in the life of someone who believes in that dream.

Chapter 3 will encourage you to let go of your own dreams and let God give you His dream for your life. This is the first practical step you will take toward becoming a dreamer.

The theme of Chapter 4 is that when God gives you a dream, He will also show you the end result of that dream. Knowing the end from the beginning is critical for getting through the inevitable tough times!

In Chapter 5 you will explore the emotional fallout of dreaming. People are usually terrified or elated when the dream sinks in, and I have learned that the way forward involves dealing with these emotional reactions according to the Word of God.

In Chapter 6 we will talk about the principle of allowing your own view of your abilities to die. Without this death a proper understanding of what God and God alone is able to do cannot spring to life in you.

The subject of Chapter 7 is the simple but significant truth that dreaming by itself is not enough. Seeing your dream through to fulfillment involves faith and hard work.

Chapter 8 is all about persevering through tough circumstances. The world around you rarely cooperates with your vision, and you will need steel in your soul to finish the race.

In Chapter 9 you will see the importance of faith and patience, which must be combined so that, with the saints of old, you might inherit what has been promised.

Chapter 10 is about the ultimate dream, which is the basis of all other dreams.

Before we go on to Chapter 2, I want to pray a prayer for you:

Father, I thank You for this dear reader.

As we look forward to Your plan for them, Lord, as Your servant I prophesy blessing and declare favor, wisdom, insight, supernatural ideas, and witty inventions for them. Lord, strategic placement at the right place and the right time and promotion come from You. Help them move their dream forward. You are faithful to show them the end from the beginning, and we are excited about that. Give them grace for the middle, because it can get tough sometimes. They know that if they will keep their eyes fixed on Jesus, on their dream, on their purpose, and on their destiny, they will have the wherewithal to move forward until that "hastily" moment is theirs and You

*have brought them to that place the dream showed them.
In Jesus' name I pray. Amen.*

THE POWER OF A DREAM

I WANT TO USE JOSEPH'S LIFE as a pattern, a sort of spiritual template for what it is to receive a dream from God and see it through to fulfillment. He was the second to the youngest son, his full brother Benjamin being the only one younger. Joseph was Jacob's favorite, and the more he favored him over his brothers, the less those brothers wanted anything to do with him.

We also saw that—after the many-colored coat fiasco— when things couldn't get any worse between the brothers, Joseph had a dream that he would be boss over all of his family. He told them about it, and that led to a whole lot more trouble for him. His older brothers threw Joseph in a pit, pondered killing him, and then decided instead to sell him as a slave. He ended up in Egypt as a servant to Potiphar, who was a high-ranking official to Pharaoh.

Joseph did very well in Potiphar's house, but then Potiphar's wife lusted after him. When he spurned her out of fear for God, she falsely accused him of rape. Joseph was cast into prison, but just as he had in Potiphar's house, he rose through the ranks and became a boss there too. In the end, Joseph's gift of interpreting dreams brought him into Pharaoh's court, and he was exalted to the position of royal vizier—lord of all Egypt under the king.

There are many lessons we can learn from this story, but again, what I want to focus on is found in Genesis 37:2. It says Joseph was seventeen years old, caring for his father's sheep. Therefore, Joseph was only seventeen when he was sold into slavery and shipped off to Egypt by his brothers. But in Genesis 41:46, in a little statement that could be lost amid all the verses about the miraculous reversal of Joseph's fortunes, it says simply, **Joseph was thirty years old when he stood before Pharaoh.**

Joseph was seventeen when he had the dream, but that dream became so much a part of him that he was able to continue moving forward toward its fulfillment through thirteen horrific, gut-wrenching years. He overcame all of his disappointment and disillusionment until his dream came to full manifestation. Now that's the power of a dream!

As we reflect on the dream of one man, it is important to embrace the idea that every one of us needs to have our own dream. What dream do you have that's going to make *someone else's* life better? What dream do you have that's going to make *your* life better? What dream do you have for a brighter future? I ask this because I want you to understand that your dream is empowering to you and to all the lives you touch.

Before we get into more about the power of your dream, let's take a look at another scripture passage about vision and accomplishment that is going to shed some light on the subject for us.

JOSHUA AND JERICHO

In Joshua, chapter 1, the Bible tells us what God said to Joshua after the death of Moses. We must remember that Moses had been Joshua's hero, his mentor, and his pastor. Joshua had watched Moses work great miracles and had been with him through the successes and the failures of the children of Israel. He had seen Moses triumph, and he had seen Moses fall.

Joshua had seen the very glory of God rest on Moses. However, by the time Moses died, no doubt the foremost thing in Joshua's mind was how Moses had been forbidden to lead God's people into the Promised Land. He watched Moses fail a critical test, which caused him to die east of the Jordan River. And, because of their whining, griping, and complaining, an entire generation of God's people was also excluded. Joshua had watched them continually fall in the wilderness over a forty-year period.

In Joshua 1 God said to him, "Joshua, Moses is dead. You're going to move forward. The past is behind you. The future is before you. Don't be afraid. Have courage! I'm going to be with you just like I was with Moses. Together we will get the job done. We're going to take My people into the Promised Land—into abundance. They will enter a land that flows with milk and honey. They will come into the blessing I have dreamed for them for a long time. And Joshua, you are going to be the one who takes them in."

Joshua was given a dream from God. God's dream for His people, the dream Moses carried all those years, was passed to Joshua. Things were all rosy at that point. Everything was fresh, exciting, and full of promise. The elders of Israel were cheering Joshua on, but then things changed. We can never stay in that wonderful, spiritual sweet spot that we were in when we first dream the dream! It doesn't work that way. It didn't with Joseph, it didn't with Joshua, and it won't with us. So pay close attention, because this is important when you think about your dream.

Even though you have a dream from the Lord—a dream that is anointed, you are excited about, and you know God has said, "I'm going to do this in you and with you and through you"—there are still going to be battles over that dream. You still have to fight for it, bear down, and participate in that dream's fulfillment. That is where Joshua was as he faced the walls of Jericho.

After some scouting and planning, in Joshua 6 we read that Joshua's leadership was put to the test as the Israelites faced their first battle in the Promised Land. The Israelites had moved into the Promised Land, but they still had to possess it, and Jericho was the first city they were to conquer. **Now Jericho was straightly shut up because of the children of Israel: none went out, and none came in. And the Lord said unto Joshua, See, I have given into thine hand Jericho, and the king thereof, and the mighty men of valour.**

And ye shall compass the city, all ye men of war, and go round about the city once. Thus shalt thou do six days. And seven priests shall bear before the ark seven trumpets of rams' horns: and the seventh day ye shall compass the city seven times, and the priests shall blow with the trumpets. And it shall come to pass, that when they make a long blast with the ram's horn, and when ye hear the sound of the trumpet, all the people shall shout with a great shout; and the wall of the city shall fall down flat, and the people shall ascend up every man straight before him (Joshua 6:1-5).

Joshua made preparations according to God's command, but just before putting his plans into action he did something significant. **And Joshua had commanded the people, saying, Ye shall not shout, nor make any noise with your voice, neither shall any word proceed out of your mouth, until the day I bid you shout; then shall ye shout** (Joshua 6:10).

Joshua had witnessed the people murmur, grumble, and complain to Moses about God, their circumstances, and about their plight in the wilderness. They whined about everything, and it cost them dearly. So Joshua said, "Now wait a minute...I'm the new leader. I saw what happened before, and I'm going to tell the people to keep their mouths shut."

Back when Joshua scouted out the Promised Land with Caleb and the other ten spies, the people freaked out over a report of giants in the land. Their response— their crying and whining and murmuring—cost those people their lives and the blessing of living in the Promised Land. Afterward, Joshua and their children weren't just facing giants. They were facing a whole city!

Joshua could hear them crying, "What's that sound? Oh, they are having chariot races on top of the wall; it is so thick and wide. And take a look at how tall that thing is! Hey, what's that speck way up at the top? That's a soldier about to spit on us. He looks so far away." Joshua knew if the first generation had been afraid of a few giants, the next generation were going to be overwhelmed by the wall, the size of the city, and the general greatness of what they were about to attack. If their mouths got them in trouble before, they could in this situation too.

Joshua did not want to fail again, so he commanded the people not to make a sound. He said, "Be quiet; don't say a word. I'll tell you when to make some noise and speak." Joshua was onto something here. We don't even have to articulate words to discourage people. Just a sneer, a grunt, or a tone of voice is enough to get a nasty attitude to rub off on folks. That's what Joshua was trying to avoid.

As he faced the formidable walls of Jericho, God prepared Joshua by saying, "I have given you the city" (Joshua 6:2, my paraphrase). He wanted Joshua to see what was going to take place in seven days—to have a vision of a desired future, His dream for Joshua. In the same way, God wants you and me to have a dream. He wants us to have dreams for different aspects of our lives: for our family, for our ministry, for our financial future, and for our church and community. God wants to stir greatness and vision in us the same way He did Joshua

In dealing with my dreams I have discovered seven points about the power a dream has in our lives. As you read about them, I want you to think about these dream powers in light of Joseph's life, Joshua's life, and the ministry of Jesus. Think about how their dreams have affected and influenced their world and yours.

POWER NUMBER ONE:
Your Dream Will Draw the Right People to You

You might think a real dream from God has enough power in it to work all on its own, just between you and God. A dream from God has a lot of power, but not that kind of power. The fact is, while we all might wish we could do life on our own, that's not how we were created. We were not designed by God for solo existence. We need other people to be happy and successful.

If you think you are going to accomplish your dream on your own, you are kidding yourself. But if you get a clear dream and vision from God, part of its power is that it is going to attract the right people to help bring it to pass. You are going to need those people. They are the ones who are going to assist you, encourage you, and support you. They are going to bless you, give to you, and counsel you through the ups and downs until the dream becomes a reality.

Jesus had a dream, a purpose, and a mission. He was the Son of God, but He also had the right people working with Him. They were drawn alongside Him. One power of a dream is that it brings the right people to you.

POWER NUMBER TWO:
Your Dream Reveals Those Not Called as Your Partners

This is a tremendous truth to grasp. Your dream will

actually repel the kind of people that will hinder you from fulfilling it. If you have a clear dream and you are going somewhere, you are excited about your future and your gaze is fixed on that goal, there may be some people who just don't want to be around you anymore. As you proceed to work out that dream, those people will drop out of the picture.

The Lord revealed to Joseph that his own brothers just did not get his dream. We read how they were repelled from Joseph. Although this was painful, God led Joseph on a path that saw his dream fulfilled. However, his brothers didn't reconnect with him until the end.

Even with Jesus, people were either attracted to Him or repelled from Him. So don't be surprised if, as you work out your dream, you are not always the most popular person on the block! Some people aren't going to get it. They are not going to understand you simply because they are not called to be a part of your dream. As a result, to some degree they are going to be repelled from you.

I'm not saying that you are going to be hated for your dreams, although it might go that far—as certainly was the case with Jesus and Joseph. But you must understand a dream's power to bring itself to pass. That power includes eliminating hindrances like people who have no understanding or appreciation for your dream.

POWER NUMBER THREE:

Your Dream Gives You Strength to Carry on in Hard Times

Speaking of Jesus, the Bible says in Hebrews 12:2, **For the joy that was set before him endured the cross, despising the shame.** Jesus had an enduring joy, and that joy was His strength (Nehemiah 8:10). The clarity of the dream His Father had given Him enabled Jesus to see that through His sacrifice, you and I would be reconciled and restored to relationship with God. That dream enabled Him to live a sinless life and to suffer being misunderstood, persecuted, mocked, unjustly tried and convicted, scourged, spat upon, and crucified. He was able to endure all of that because He had a dream. His dream gave Him the stuff to see things through to the end.

I have experienced this same strength and perseverance in carrying out my dream. After I had worked in California for a year, in February of 1982 I started my church in a lady's living room. A year later we had fourteen people. About that time I called my folks in Illinois. When my dad got on the phone, I said, "We had fourteen people on Thursday night!"

My dad said, "Son, do you want me to send you some money so you can come home?" He was concerned about me, but I was totally oblivious to the fact that having only people fourteen was not great. It was great to me! After all, God had multiplied the church fourteen times!

My dream was giving me the spiritual stamina to carry on and have joy in hard times.

Joseph ended up in prison, but he kept his attitude right because he had a dream that empowered him to do so. He knew what God had shown him. He had faith God was going to bring it to pass because part of the power of a dream is imparting a supernatural strength to overcome the trials you suffer while seeing the dream through. In the same way your dream will give you the wherewithal to cheerfully move forward even in times of difficulty.

POWER NUMBER FOUR:
Your Dream Provides Hope for a Better Future

My own desire is that you are a hopeful, positive person, who has a dream of something better in your future. Certainly, when you think about the days to come, you shouldn't be thinking things are going to get worse and worse because God's Word says, **But the path of the just is as the shining light, that shineth more and more unto the perfect day** (Proverbs 4:18).

If you have a tendency to think negatively and hopelessly about days to come, you need to back up and say, "Lord, I know You want to give me a hope for a better future. You want to give me a dream of something better, of going higher with You and walking with You in a greater dimension. You want to give me an exciting life that's filled with Your supernatural intervention, joy, wisdom, and power. I want to receive all that now! Thank You for giving me a dream that stirs my soul and ignites my spirit."

Jeremiah 29:11 THE MESSAGE says, **I have it all planned out—plans to take care of you, not abandon you, plans to give you the future you hope for.** Any dream birthed by the Holy Spirit in your heart will empower you to see things clearly. It will destroy confusion and doubt. It even has the power to break depression off your life. God's dream for your life will provide a sense of hope for a brighter and a better future.

POWER NUMBER FIVE
Your Dream Has the Power to Change the Atmosphere and the Culture

Think about the life of Jesus. Although His dream seemed unlikely to the Pharisees and the Sadducees and the other skeptics of His day, it revolutionized the world. What Jesus did redeemed humanity, providing a way for us to return to our original position and state of being with God.

Think about the life of Dr. Martin Luther King Jr. His dream changed our nation, altering our culture and political atmosphere. Our dreams can too! Our lives may not have the far-reaching impact of Jesus or Martin Luther King Jr., but they can make a difference in people's lives, bringing change in the atmosphere and quality of life.

Before Joshua went into Canaan, it was a place of idolatry and wickedness. It was so wicked God sent Joshua to conquer rather than convert. But his dream changed the atmosphere of the land. With his conquest came the knowledge of God. The evil culture was overturned, and the land was renewed. Your dream has within it the power to conquer what opposes you and dispel darkness with light!

POWER NUMBER SIX:

Your Dream Provides Proper Priorities and Parameters

One of the things I appreciate about having a clear vision is that it makes so many decisions for me. Over time it just winnows out all the peripheral, unnecessary stuff and gives me a clear sense of direction. This also eliminates a whole lot of decision making. I don't have to struggle with, "Well, should I do this?" or "Should I do that?" I know I am going somewhere, and I have to invest all my energy and my time in moving that dream forward. I cannot and will not be sidetracked if I can help it.

When Nehemiah was rebuilding the city of Jerusalem after it had been sacked and burned, two men by the names of Sanballat and Geshem tried to get him to stop the work (Nehemiah 6:1-3. They said, "Hey Nehemiah, come down into the plain of Ono, and let's have lunch together."

Nehemiah answered, "Sorry guys, but I can't come down. The work I'm doing is too important. I have to stay focused on the rebuilding effort." The dream God gave Nehemiah exposed all the distractions and nonsense of his world and his life, and your dream has the power to provide proper priorities and parameters so you can live simply and successfully also.

POWER NUMBER SEVEN:
Your Dream Fosters Insights and Creative Solutions

Part of the inherent power of your dream from God is that it produces in you the creativity you need to accomplish it. As you press forward, insights and ideas will begin to flow into your heart, your mind, and your awareness. You will have the tools for and the creative solutions to problems that arise.

A fine example is Joshua at the battle of Jericho, where God gave a word of wisdom to him. Joshua had a problem on his hands—a crowd of people with a history of saying things that got them into trouble. The stakes couldn't be higher, and he couldn't afford another plague from God because they grieved His Spirit with doubt and unbelief toward His promises.

As Joshua faced this problem, the creative solution bubbled up from his heart to tell the people to be silent until he gave the signal. But, in the meantime, "Shhh." Shhh? What kind of solution was that? "My feet hurt!" Shhh. "I'm tired!" Shhh. "I don't know if..." Shhh! At the right time Joshua commanded, "Shout!" And the walls came tumbling down, all because of a simple but effective idea that Joshua's dream produced in him. The power of a dream is increased creativity to bring that dream about.

VISIONARY DREAMING

I heard that in the last days of Smith Wigglesworth (a great man of God who lived in England years ago), few came to visit him. It saddens me greatly that the younger generation of leaders and believers in the church didn't glean from this great man of God's wisdom and experience. For that reason, every month I personally visit Oral Roberts. I don't worship any human being, but I do appreciate the greatness of a man like him. He's had a tremendous influence on this nation and upon the church because he has changed our perspective of who God is and how God wants to move in our lives. Knowing all that, I don't want him to go to Heaven without sitting at his feet as often as I can.

Each month I take a group of pastors and other ministers to see Brother Roberts. Once he said, "If there was one parting thing I could say, it would be that even though we are not called to be Jesus, and we can't be Jesus, still we are called to be like Him. When you read the Gospels and about the life of Jesus, think about how Jesus saw people, about His perspective and how He loved even the unlovely—those who were sinful, those who were not church members, those who were not pretty and those who were pretty, those who were down and out and those who were up and out, and those who were impoverished and those who were wealthy—just think about how He loved humankind, how He perceived them. Then think about how people perceived Him. Again, we can't be Jesus, but we can be like Him."

Brother Roberts concluded, "So then, do your best to be like Jesus, to look at people like He looked at people, and let people look to you like Jesus let people look to Him. Let your dream be not only about being blessed yourself, but let your dream be about being a blessing in His name."

That's the kind of dream to have! Brother Roberts was talking about a dream like Martin Luther King Jr.'s, Joseph's, or Joshua's. The apostle Paul had a dream to establish strong churches, a dream many believers past and present have had. Think about Mary the mother of Jesus. God gave her a dream that changed all of our lives forever. What a dream she let God dream through her!

Let your dream not only bring blessing and refreshing to you, but let it also bring hope and help to a world that is hurting and in great need.

Father, I believe in the core of my being that every one of us desires to have a dream that is birthed by Your Spirit in our hearts and minds. Like the apostle Paul, we want to apprehend that for which we have been apprehended of Christ. We are not here by accident. You have a design, a purpose, a hope, a calling, and a dream for every one of us. Our goal is to dream Your dream for us.

When we have Your dream, Father, when we become aware of that dream and can articulate it, we trust it will draw the right people to us, repel the wrong people from us, and give us tenacity and an enduring hope. The dream You birthed in our hearts will change the atmosphere around us, give us a sense of priorities and parameters, and we will have new creativity to fulfill that dream.

Father, I pray for the one reading these words, that they would have a clearer understanding and a fuller picture of Your dream for their life. Help them to touch a hurting world. In Jesus' name we pray. Amen.

LET GOD GIVE YOU
YOUR DREAM

I HAVE CHALLENGED YOU TO DREAM, and you have explored the power of a dream. We have looked at Joseph as a model for successful dreaming, reading that he received his dream when he was only seventeen years old but waited thirteen years as a slave and prisoner in Egypt before his dream became a reality.

In this chapter I'm going to talk about how we should allow God to give us a dream. If we want a dream that will move forward until it is fulfilled, we need to let God be the one to plant that dream within us in the first place. When God is involved in our dreams, it will stretch us! We will come to depend completely on His supernatural infusion of power.

God has a dream for every person. In fact, the Bible says if we will embrace God's dream, it will be exceeding and abundantly above all we can ask or think for ourselves. You might say, "Amen, Pastor Jeff! I want God's dream for my life! Hallelujah!" But letting God give you a dream is more of an issue than you might think. It is very important to understand that you might very well have a dream for your life that isn't necessarily God's dream.

I had my own dreams for my life. When I was eighteen years old I wanted to be a banker. I didn't want to be a preacher. I was moving forward in my dream, and I was totally focused on it. I already worked in a bank and planned to go to the junior college in my home town of Mattoon, Illinois, because they had a banking degree program. I was developing relationships with bank presidents and other important people in the area. I wanted to be a community leader like Charles E. White, president of Mattoon Bank, who lent people money to buy a new home or a new car. I dreamed of helping other people realize their dreams—that was my vision as a young man.

I also loved the Lord. When my mom and dad went on vacation, I had some time in the house by myself, and I had this thought, *Well, I better check with God and make sure my dream is His dream.* I prayed, "Okay Lord, I have some great plans for me, but I just want to make sure this is all okay with You. I'm about to finish high school and launch into my life, and I want to know I've heard from You and this is all good."

As I prayed and spent time with the Lord, I started to sense a call on my life to ministry. The more I prayed, the more I knew it was ministry. I was aggravated! To be honest, I was upset with the Lord because I had a plan for myself that was wonderful and He was about to mess it up. I said, "Okay Lord, if You want me to be a preacher, I'll do it on weekends."

I was thinking along these lines because the Full Gospel Business Men's Fellowship was big at that time. They are an organization of businessmen who meet regularly to share the Lord and invite their business friends and colleagues to their lunch or dinner meetings as an evangelistic outreach. I learned from them that I could be a business person and still minister.

"That's what I'll do. I'll be a businessman and preach on the weekends." I was willing to sacrifice my weekends, but then I heard God say, "I don't want your sacrifice." The Bible says, **To obey is better than sacrifice** (1 Samuel 15: 22). He wanted obedience from me, not my attempts to work things out so I could have it both ways.

I tried something else. I said, "Okay Lord, if I go into the ministry, I know I don't want to be a pastor. I want to be an evangelist!" I used to watch R.W. Schambach and Jimmy Swaggart and just be enthralled. I would go to a Jimmy Swaggart meeting, he would come to the platform with that leather satchel, and I would think, "Oh man,

I don't know what's in there, but that's cool. Boy, is that ever cool."

The tent evangelist thing was before my time, but I somehow plugged into it. I imagined how they would introduce me as the preacher. "And now at this time, it is my distinct privilege and pleasure to introduce to you the man God has chosen to spearhead miracle revival across the nation and around the world, God's man of faith and power, Jeff Walker!" I wanted to blow into a town, blow up the town, and blow out of that town. I didn't want to stay in one place and have the responsibility of a lot of people—my job description of a pastor.

Eventually I did let God give me His dream for my life, and I have had a wonderful, fruitful ministry as a result. But I have to say something here. A lot of times we get the impression that if God really wants to use us, He's going to call us into full-time ministry. That just isn't so. Remember Pastor Joe Bergeron from Chapter 1, the one who told me I should go to Palm Springs and start a church? His story is very interesting.

Joe and I had been in Bible college together, and even back then he used to tell me, "You know, Jeff, I wanted to be a doctor. I could have been a doctor, and I should have been a doctor. I'm smart enough to be a doctor, and I know that because I went to Cal State for a year and found out I have the intelligence to be a doctor."

All through our time at school, Joe talked about what he should have, could have, would have, and ought to have done about being a doctor.

After pastoring Burbank Faith Center for several years, Joe came on staff with me as an associate pastor. We sent him on annual mission trips to India for several years, and he would come back from India saying, "I should have been a doctor. If I were a doctor, I could treat these people and their sicknesses with simple medical treatments that would make a dramatic difference in their lives. I could preach the gospel and minister to them through medicine. If only I had been a doctor!"

Finally, after eleven long years of listening to his whining, I said, "Joe, for years you have been in ministry saying 'I could have been a doctor. I should have been a doctor. I wish I was a doctor.' Why don't you become a doctor?"

At thirty years old Joe went back to finish his bachelor's degree, then got accepted into medical school, and now he is a doctor. He established his medical practice in Indianapolis, Indiana, and married an East Indian woman. They go to India regularly, doing medical missions and preaching, and he is happy and content. He's fulfilled because God's dream for his life was not for him to be a preacher but to use his gifts in a non-typical full-time ministry. We are all in ministry, but God's dream for Joe was to minister to people as a medical doctor.

Don't discount yourself if God calls you to be a welder or an accountant or a school teacher. At your welding shop, your office, or your classroom, you are going to be able to touch people's lives who don't want to go to church to hear a preacher. They wouldn't come to my church to hear me, so God placed you in their lives, letting the life of Jesus shine through you. You have a voice into their world. Be open! God may call you to any number of professions in order to reach the lost.

Look at the people in the Bible who built the temple. All of the curtains, furniture, lavers, and every utensil had to be made just the right way. The people who made these things were called by God and anointed with His Spirit for what we would call manual labor, and sometimes it was pretty mundane. Nevertheless, it was God's anointed work—and it was extremely important to Him!

Do not allow the enemy to run you down, and don't discount yourself from your part in God's plan. His dream for your life is powerful, whether it is done in the limelight or in the shadows. The main point is to let God give you your dream. To make it a little easier, I want to share seven ways you can receive the dream God has for you.

NUMBER ONE:
You Should Be Moved by Compassion

Very often, what moves you to compassion is a real

indicator of God's dream for your life. What stirs you to compassion is very revealing and telling. Five times in the Gospels the Bible says, "Jesus was moved with compassion," twice Jesus said, "I feel compassion," and three times He included compassion in parables as an ideal of God's attitude toward people. Jesus was compelled to help people, to reach out to the hurting because He was moved with compassion. Jesus talked about the significance of compassion. We are to have His compassion for others and are to be moved by it.

Looking back at Joseph in Egypt, when he revealed himself to his brothers who had betrayed him, he did it with forgiveness and compassion. **Then Joseph could not refrain himself before all them that stood by him; and he cried, Cause every man to go out from me. And there stood no man with him, while Joseph made himself known unto his brethren. And he wept aloud: and the Egyptians and the house of Pharaoh heard. And Joseph said unto his brethren, I am Joseph; doth my father yet live? And his brethren could not answer him; for they were troubled at his presence. And Joseph said unto his brethren, Come near to me, I pray you. And they came near. And he said, I am Joseph your brother, whom ye sold into Egypt. Now therefore be not grieved, nor angry with yourselves, that ye sold me hither: for God did send me before you to preserve life (Genesis 45:1-5).**

Although this happened after Joseph's dream had come to full manifestation, God had seen Joseph's heart and knew how he would respond to being mistreated and then receiving great authority. When he was seventeen surely Joseph didn't say to himself, "I want to be a slave in Egypt for the next thirteen years. Then I will gain the compassion and wisdom I need to rule." No, God altered the path of Joseph's dream to incite compassion in him. Compassion is the stuff that God's dreams are made of.

Do yourself a great favor by letting God dream His dream through you, even if that means He may interrupt your dream as you move toward it. And the way he may interrupt it is by stirring and awaking compassion in you in an area that doesn't have anything to do with what you have been thinking.

NUMBER TWO:
You Should Pay Attention to What Frustrates You

Moses was frustrated by how the Egyptians oppressed his people. Jesus was frustrated with the dead Pharisaic religion and how it spiritually bankrupted the people He ministered to. Martin Luther King Jr. was frustrated by racial inequality. All of them moved according to the dream God gave them to change things, a pattern we see over and over in the Word of God.

Look at the apostle Paul, for example. False teachers and prophets frustrated him. Not only was he compelled by compassion and love, but he was also frustrated, aggravated, and fed up by the nonsense that was going on with his spiritual children. He would lead these baby Christians to Christ and get them born into the family of God, and then people would rush right in and put them under legalistic bondage to a bunch of rules and regulations that had nothing to do with New Testament Christianity. This really infuriated Paul.

An illustration of this was the Galatians. They had received Christ and were growing in the love of God as they headed for Heaven. Then these people came to them and said, "You know, if you really want to be in God's family, you still need to be circumcised. Jesus was a *Jewish* Messiah and you have to keep the Jewish law to qualify for what He did for you."

Paul hated legalism, or putting people under the law. You can feel the aggravation and the fire in his belly when he says, "If these folks who are stirring up this trouble think circumcision is so great, why don't they just go all the way and castrate themselves? Then they would really be holy!" That's exactly what he said in Galatians 5:12. After Paul's letter to the Galatians, there weren't any more problems in that area!

If we go further back in the Old Testament, we read how Nehemiah was frustrated by the fact that his beloved home city of Jerusalem and the Jewish Temple lay in ruins. His frustration was part of the dream that drove him to restore everything. Although you probably wouldn't call it frustration, Joseph was certainly concerned for the people when he heard Pharaoh's dream about the impending famine. Confronting a potential humanitarian disaster, God gave him the vision of a solution.

You can tell when you are moved with love and compassion toward hurting humanity whose circumstances and situations are unrighteous. There is a divine discontent that stirs in your heart and points you to your purpose. This is biblical! You can find examples of both compassion and frustration leading to great dreams throughout the Scriptures.

NUMBER THREE:
Sometimes You Find Your Dream by Helping Someone Else in Theirs

Jesus said something powerful, **If therefore ye have not been faithful in the unrighteous mammon, who will commit to your trust the true riches? And if ye have not been faithful in that which is another man's, who shall give you that which is your own?** (Luke 16:11-12).

Think of Elijah and Elisha, those great Old Testament prophets. Elijah had wonderful miracles, signs, and prophetic utterance in his ministry. Then he took on an assistant named Elisha. Elisha fell in love with the ministry of being a prophet by following after Elijah, partnering with him, serving him, and assisting him. The Bible says he **poured water on the hands of Elijah** (2 Kings 3:11). He was so faithful, when Elijah got ready to pass from the scene, in 2 Kings 2:9 he said to him, "Is there anything I can do for you?"

Elisha answered, "I want a double portion of the anointing of God on you. I want to follow in your footsteps. I want to be like you." Elisha had found his dream by participating in Elijah's.

Elijah didn't make it easy for Elisha, but in the end he got what he asked for. The way he did it was by staying close to Elijah, ministering to him, and making sure his dream was happening. By sticking to his side, he saw Elijah carried up to Heaven by the chariot of fire, and he got Elijah's mantle—with a double portion of God's anointing.

The special mentor-disciple relationship between Elijah and Elisha may not always be available to you, but the principle still matters. If you serve another person in their God-given vision and consider it important because it is something from God, God will honor you and bring a dream into your life.

NUMBER FOUR:

You Can Find Your Dream by Spending Time in God's Word

Did you know that Jesus found Himself in the Bible? We know this because of the way He was raised. We know because of His encounter with the priests in the Temple when He was twelve. He had all the answers to their questions. Then Mary and Joseph came to get Him because He had not been with them when they began the journey back to Nazareth. He said to them, **I must be about my Father's business** (Luke 2:49). He knew from reading the Word that He was the Son of God.

We also know Jesus read about Himself in God's Word because when He started His public ministry, He read this from the scroll of Isaiah in the synagogue in Nazareth, **The Spirit of the Lord is upon Me because He has anointed Me** (Luke 4:18). It was a powerful moment of self-realization when He said, "Hey, here I am. That's Me." Having found Himself in the Scriptures, He was able to clearly define His goals and articulate His dream.

I hope you find yourself in the Bible, because you are in there. "I am?" you might ask. It says, **These signs shall follow them that believe** (Mark 16:17). Do you believe? Unfortunately, most believers are following signs when signs are supposed to follow them! There is a big meeting in town, and Reverend Steve Stunning is there every night, in person, healing people, delivering people, and getting people saved. So we just run after the signs when signs are supposed to follow us.

If you are a believer as you read this, you are in the Bible. When it says signs and wonders shall follow those who believe, it means you will pray for hurting people, reach out with God's healing touch, and be moved by His compassion. The Lord will help you to finely tune your dream if you will spend time in His Word.

Jesus said, **If ye continue in my word, then are ye my disciples indeed; And ye shall know the truth, and the truth shall make you free** (John 8:31-32). The Bible also says that the entrance of God's Word gives us light (Psalm 119:130). If you want God to give you a dream for your life or you need clarification of your vision, read and study His Word! When God's Word comes into your heart and mind, it will bring the light to see your life the way He does.

NUMBER FIVE:
Sometimes God Will Give You a Dream by Supernatural Intervention

Even though I have been talking about dreams and visions in the sense of inner purpose and life direction, there is no reason to limit God. Like Joseph in the book of Genesis, He may give you a literal dream as you are sleeping. Like Mary the mother of Jesus, He may send an angel to speak to you about your life. Perhaps He will communicate through the gifts of the Holy Spirit. Or He might supernaturally confirm the dream He has placed in your heart through the preaching of the Word, solidifying and sealing it in your heart.

Joel 2: 28 says, **And it shall come to pass afterward, that I will pour out my spirit upon all flesh; and your sons and your daughters shall prophesy, your old men shall dream dreams, your young men shall see visions.** This is God's promise, generally given to the church, that He will send supernatural gifts to bless His people. And He has been true to that promise. He has visited many people in a variety of ways to show them something. The key is not to have any preconceptions or put Him in a box, expecting Him to reveal your dream this way or that way. If you seek Him and desire His dream, He will reveal it His way, which is the whole point.

At the same time, don't be discouraged if the angel Gabriel doesn't show up in your kitchen! You need to have faith in the Lord and trust Him. Believe He can speak to you any way He wants to. Just because you never had an angelic visitation, a literal dream in the night, or a supernatural intervention, that does not diminish or discount your life dream. God guides you in many ways, and following Him is what matters.

NUMBER SIX:

Wise Counsel Facilitates Your Dream

The Bible says, **Where no counsel is, the people fall: but in the multitude of counselors there is safety** (Proverbs 11:14). It also says, **Without counsel purposes are disappointed: but in the multitude of counselors they are established** (Proverbs 15:22). We want safety, and we want our purposes to be established and not disappointed.

In His wisdom God has determined that His voice can be heard through the counsel of people who have more experience than we do, who might be in authority over us in the Lord, and who have a special love for us because they know and care about us. There are many visions and dreams that need to be guided by wise counsel, sometimes because they are way off, and sometimes because they just need to be adjusted a little bit. There is safety and success in wise counsel.

Along with this comes the need for wisdom in how we share our vision. We need to be careful who we share our dreams with and when. Joseph, in his youthful impetuosity, blew it on both counts. He prematurely shared his dream with the wrong people (his brothers), and then he found out their opinion on the dream (Genesis 37:8, my paraphrase). "Who do you think you are? So, you have a big dream that we are going to serve you, eh? Well, we'll show you what's going to happen"—and they stripped him of his coat of many colors and threw him in a pit! Then they sold him into slavery. In the end he found himself in jail, and his brothers were saying the whole time, "Now what do you think about your little dream, Dreamer Joe the Wonder Boy?"

T. L. Osborn, a great apostle of God, once said, "You know, you have to be really careful about letting people's opinion influence you and your self-perception. One time I was preaching and someone came up to me and said, 'Brother Osborn! Brother Osborn! You are more like Jesus than any human being I have ever met! You look like Jesus, you talk like Jesus, your beautiful eyes radiate the love of Jesus, and your gorgeous beard just reminds me of Jesus. You remind me of Jesus so much that I just wanted to thank you for being a reflection of Him.' I felt so good about that.

"Then a few weeks later I was preaching in another city and someone came up after the service and said, 'Mr. Osborn, I want you to know that you remind me more of the devil than anyone I ever met. Your red hair—and especially that beard—really look like the devil, and even the things you say remind me of the devil.' So much for going by what people think of us!"

This is an important point and a fine distinction. When you begin to have a dream, and you are able to see that dream more and more clearly and articulate it, wise counsel is priceless. It can make the difference between a passing fancy and building something that lasts forever. At the same time, be very careful not to become a collector of opinions. There is a vast difference between getting wise counsel for something you believe in and collecting people's opinions because you want or need their support for its own sake.

NUMBER SEVEN:
God Will Develop Your Dream by Working in You

Philippians 2:13 is one of my favorite verses because it speaks of God working in you. It doesn't matter whether you are young or old, rich or poor, educated or uneducated. The Bible teaches that all those divisions and classifications just break down before God. He loves us all the same. He seeks to lift the poor and the weak as well as the rich and the strong and establish us all in Him.

No matter what station of life you may find yourself occupying, God wants to give you a dream. He promises to work in you, stir you, mold and shape your expectations and your sense of purpose. He wants to work **in you both to will and to do of his good pleasure** (Philippians 2:13). Your dream will take shape and unfold inside of you even as you move forward in Him.

Jesus told this particular parable about a sower in Mark 4:26-27. He said, **So is the kingdom of God, as if a** man should cast seed into the ground; And should sleep, and rise night and day, and the seed should spring and grow up, he knoweth not how. God's dream will work in you as you rest in Him and move forward, faithfully obeying His Spirit. Your dream will take on a life of its own as you follow Him.

PITFALLS FOR THE DREAMER

There is something all of us can do—that I have done but didn't want to do—when it comes to dreaming. What I refer to is cloaking our opinions and dreams in God as if they were His. We attribute our opinion to God, but it is really what we think and dream. This is a real danger! We don't want *our* opinion, even dressed up in Jesus. We want *His* opinion. And when it comes to other folks' dreams, we want discerning and wise hearts insofar as their dream might affect us.

Jeremiah 23:25 says, I have heard what the prophets said, that prophesy lies in my name, saying, I have dreamed, I have dreamed. If someone really has a dream from God, it is going to bear out over time and be fruitful. Sometimes we have to back up like they did in Acts 5:38-39 and say, "Well, if this is God, it is going to last. No sense in trying to stop it. And if it is not of God, it is going to fail anyway. So we don't need to do anything about it."

When people say, "I have a dream," and your spirit doesn't bear witness with it, just back away, let them do their thing, and see how it works out. I'm not talking about having a bad attitude about it, but if you have questions in your spirit or their words don't quite resonate with you, just watch and see what happens. That's wise counsel.

Jeremiah goes on to say in 23:30-32, **Therefore, behold, I am against the prophets, saith the Lord, that steal my words every one from his neighbour. Behold, I am against the prophets, saith the Lord, that use their tongues, and say, He saith. Behold, I am against them that prophesy false dreams, saith the Lord, and do tell them, and cause my people to err by their lies, and by their lightness; yet I sent them not, nor commanded them: therefore they shall not profit this people at all, saith the Lord.**

This is a powerful passage. It is loaded with a serious message about how to hear from God, stay real, and identify falsehood in yourself and others. It says God is against dream stealers and people who cloak their own ideas with the name of God when God hasn't said a thing.

My dad's brother passed a few years ago, but before that he lived in St. Louis. Uncle Mark worked for a large engineering firm, but he had earned a theological doctorate and was also a preacher. He led a street ministry, feeding the hungry and homeless, and did a lot of work with prison release programs. He had genuine compassion for these people. He also had a ministry of intercession, and he prayed for me every single day. About once a month he would call—especially the last few years before he passed—and say, "I'm praying for you. I want you to know that the Lord tells me you are an original. Don't try to be like anyone else, because you are an original."

That is what the Bible teaches! You are an original and should not try to be like everyone else. If you share your dream and people say, "Whoa, that is weird"—don't let it get you down. When Dr. Paul Yonggi Cho started his work in Seoul, Korea, many people (particularly in America) thought, "Well, that cell group thing just won't work." Today, approximately 800,000 members later, Americans are saying, "Uh, how does that cell group stuff work?" Dr. Cho has the largest church on the Earth. So dream your dream, and if people don't like it, they can lump it. Be an original.

Then God says He's not against prophesying a dream, but He is against us prophesying a dream we have thought up and attributed to Him. It is important for us to pray, "Lord, I don't want to articulate my own dream. Although it might be good, I want You to give me Your dream. Let me have Your purpose and passion for accomplishment in my life." If we pray that and mean it, we won't be presenting our own plans as if they were from God.

Jeremiah also said in verse 32 that false prophets prophesy **by their lightness**. What does that mean? We should not be frivolous with "God said." How often do we say, "the Lord showed me," "the Lord told me," "the Lord said to wear the pink dress today," or "the Lord told me to go to this store"? I know the Lord speaks to us, and the Holy Spirit wants to guide every aspect of our lives. But be careful. Don't attribute things to the Lord lightly.

Oral Roberts said the Lord has spoken to him only about forty times in almost seventy years of ministry. I know a lot of Charismatic pastors who say the Lord speaks to them about forty times before breakfast and then changes His mind during the day! Again, I believe God can and does speak to us, but we should not be light about attributing things to Him. We are to be sober, serious, sincere, and wise. God will bring His reality to us.

Father, we want Your dream, Your purpose, Your plan, Your wisdom, Your counsel, and Your guidance for our future. Some of us have wonderful dreams, while some of us never have had anything clearly articulated. Whatever our situation, we open ourselves to You. If You have something else or something more for us to dream, we give ourselves to You. We bow our hearts before you. We yield ourselves and say, "Not our will, Lord, but Your will be done in us and through us." Give us a dream that is deeply rooted in Your dream of touching a hurting world and reconciling humanity to Yourself. We know You are faithful to complete the good work You have begun in us. In Jesus' name we pray. Amen.

GOD SHOWS YOU
THE END AT THE BEGINNING

IN HEBREWS 11 THE BIBLE talks about the lives of the men and women of the Old Testament. It describes how they ran their race, finished their course, did great things for God, and saw His divine intervention in their lives and in their world. Then, in Hebrews 12:1 it says, **Wherefore seeing we also are compassed about with so great a cloud of witnesses, let us lay aside every weight, and the sin which doth so easily beset us, and let us run with patience the race that is set before us.**

God is telling us, "Think about those who have gone before you, and how they have become a great cloud of witnesses." He tells us there are those who have gone before us who dreamed their dreams, who fulfilled their purposes and accomplished their ministries, and now they are cheering us on from the grandstands of Heaven. The point is, the spiritual realm is like a stadium, and these faithful ones ran and completed their races. Now they are cheering us on to dream and finish our races.

How do we do this? Hebrews 12:2 tells us how. **Looking unto Jesus the author and the finisher of our faith.** If Jesus is the author of our dreams, this is really good news! It means He will be the finisher of our dreams too. We participate and bring what we have to the table, but He will finish our dreams in us and through us.

The Bible goes on to say, **who for the joy that was set before him endured the cross, despising the shame, and is set down at the right hand of the throne of God. For consider him that endured such contradiction of sinners against himself, lest ye be wearied and faint in your minds** (Hebrews 2-3). This passage reveals one of the great keys to successful dreaming in God. We are to look to Jesus because He serves as a model for what our understanding and attitudes should be. It also shows the effect that a clear vision of the final result has upon someone who gets a dream from God.

When we think about getting weary and giving up, we need to look to Jesus and see how He dreamed His dream and ran His race. We need to see that when things got tough, it was for the joy set before Him that He completed His calling and saw it through. What was His joy? You and I! We were Jesus' dream, which was the Father's dream in Him. God dreamed of us being reconciled to Him, and He cast that vision through Jesus.

It was the sheer force and power of God's dream, of envisioning us standing as His children in Paradise, that empowered Jesus to face **the contradiction of sinners**. It helped Him get past their grumbling and doubting. It helped Him overcome the false accusations and criticism. And in the end it helped Him through His sufferings when they pulled out His beard, spat in His face, scourged Him, and hung Him on the Cross to die. Jesus endured all of that because He had a clear and powerful vision. He had a dream that showed Him the end from the beginning.

A characteristic of every true dream from God is that the dream shows us the end at the beginning. Stephen Covey says basically the same thing in his book *Seven Habits of Highly Effective People*. In his book, "Habit #2" is beginning with the end in mind, which is right out of the Bible. That is exactly what God has been doing for thousands of years! He had a firm idea of what light was going to be when He said, "Light be." He had an idea of what we were going to look like when He began to form and shape us in His image. In other words, He had a dream, He knew the end at the beginning, and He moved towards that end.

There are vital principles involved in knowing the end from the beginning when it comes to your dream.

Just like Jesus had a dream and saw the end even at the beginning, you need to see the end at the beginning as well. You need to know what that knowledge and vision will do in you.

PRINCIPLE NUMBER ONE:
Knowing the End Enables You to Maintain Your Goal in the Middle

As we have seen, Joseph had a dream of a certain end result. He saw himself being a great leader, God's instrument to bring help and hope in desperate times. He saw himself carrying out a divine purpose, being effective for God's kingdom and helping hurting humanity. This was the end result he saw for himself.

At the age of seventeen, by the power of the Spirit Joseph stood at the beginning and looked at the end. However, before Joseph saw all that become reality, he had to pass through a very difficult "middle time." He was sold by his brothers to slave traders, carried off to Egypt, became a slave in Potiphar's house, and was tempted to sin. When he didn't sin he was falsely accused and thrown into prison, where he spent many years. It was a difficult middle time, but as he went through thirteen tough years of being misunderstood—with no one believing in his dream or thinking he was going to amount to anything—Joseph was able to hold on and keep pursuing the dream in his heart. How? He had seen the end at the beginning.

I have a vision for the direction of my ministry and my church. I see it in my spirit, and I envision it. I see where my church is going. This has nothing to do with New Age thinking because I didn't come up with this dream nor did the enemy. God did. He has made this very real to me. In my spirit I see thousands of wonderful people receiving Christ. I see this desert flourishing spiritually, and I see spiritual confusion being dispelled. I envision God being glorified and Jesus being exalted.

It just so happens that right now I'm in the middle place. This doesn't mean that I'm not enjoying life in ministry and in the Lord. I'm just saying that sometimes our dreams chap our hide a little! It can frustrate us, and we will ask, "Why not sooner?" or "Why not now?" The "going through" process of the dream can be hard on our flesh and our soul. Whether we struggle with the daily grind of sticking with it or face terrible trials like Joseph, if we see the end at the beginning we can press through the hard middle time to see our dreams fulfilled.

Principle Number Two:
Knowing the End Gives You an Inner Anchor

Habakkuk 2:2-3 says, **And the Lord answered me, and said, Write the vision, and make it plain upon tables, that he may run that readeth it. For the vision is yet for an** appointed time, but at the end it shall speak, and not lie: though it tarry, wait for it; because it will surely come, it will not tarry.

This passage assures us that, although completing the vision and fulfilling the dream may take longer than we first think, knowing the end from the beginning gives us something to anchor ourselves to. Knowing the end from the beginning gives us the ability to write the vision down. Then we can refer to it and show it to others so they can appreciate it and tie into it. If it is clear, even others can support us along the way.

Consider the saying, "Your dream may sometimes feel out of reach, but it should never be out of sight." In other words, even if you cannot accomplish your dream right now in your own power, at the snap of your fingers, that doesn't mean it has to be or should be unclear to you. Wherever you are in the unfolding of your dream, it should be clear in your heart and mind—clear enough to write down. That clarity serves as a point of reference you can return to when things get foggy and the going gets tough.

In the early days of my ministry, before I ever moved to California or became a pastor, the Lord spoke to me that radio would be part of the ministry of my church. I was convinced then, and still am, that God is the author of that dream and will be the finisher of it too. It was so clear and real to me that I got a picture of a radio station and have always kept it on a wall in my office. One day a businessman came to see me. He saw the picture and asked, "What's that?"

I said, "It's a radio station."

He said, "Does this church have a radio station?"

I said, "No, but we are going to."

Because of the clarity of that vision he helped us build a tower facility and other things needed for the operation of a radio station, totaling over a million dollars of blessing for our church. All that came just because of a picture on the wall! We didn't have a fifty-page document, a detailed business plan, or a budget for a radio station, but the picture provided a real reference point and an anchor for me and other people like that businessman to tie ourselves to.

The same type of thing happened with my education. I had a dream and a desire to attend Oral Roberts University. I didn't have any idea how I was going to get to ORU, because I was pastoring in Palm Springs, but that was my dream. I went to visit the prayer tower at ORU, and while I was there I bought myself an ORU alumni mug. I hadn't taken a class there, much less graduated, but that mug sat on my desk for ten years. When ORU alumni saw it, they would ask, "Are you an ORU alumnus?"

"No," I would say. "Just got the mug."

"Well, did you attend ORU?"

"No, but I did go there and buy the mug."

Eventually I found out about a modular education program at ORU that allowed me to take classes by going there one week a month for five years. Through these classes I finished my master's and doctoral degrees. So now I am an ORU alumnus, with all the rights privileges granted thereto, including drinking out of the mug!

Knowing the end from the beginning gives us an enduring focus that serves as an anchor—something we can always refer to. And having something written or tangible, like my mug or my picture of a radio station, enables us to continue to move toward the fulfillment of our dreams.

PRINCIPLE NUMBER THREE:
Knowing the End Helps You Assess Where You Are

If you are going to go somewhere, it is important to know where you are now. My wife drives a car that's equipped with a GPS locator. It's a device that connects to a satellite that has a bird's-eye view of the Earth and knows where the car is in relation to where it is going. All you have to do is punch in your destination, and the machine tells you where to go until you arrive.

Your dream is like that GPS locator. You know where you are now because it is what you are currently experiencing. You know where you are going because your dream shows you the end from the beginning. By comparing the two, you are able to see your progress and make an assessment about your current position.

Paul's big picture and vision was a lifetime pursuit of God, which he articulated in Philippians 3:12, **I follow after, if that I may apprehend that for which also I am apprehended of Christ Jesus.** That's the end, his goal. But it is that goal that helps Paul see where he is now, as he says in Philippians 3:13, **Brethren, I count not myself to have apprehended.** Paul knows his vision, and he knows he is not there yet. This realization helps him assess his progress and come up with a personal strategy, which he declares in Philippians 3:13-14, **But this one thing I do, forgetting those things which are behind, and reaching forth unto those things which are before, I press toward the mark for the prize of the high calling of God in Christ Jesus.**

The "inner GPS" that Paul's dream granted him gave him strength and motivation to strive for its complete fulfillment.

PRINCIPLE NUMBER FOUR:
Knowing the End Tells You If You Are Going in the Right Direction

If you have your ladder leaning against the wrong building, you may be climbing, but you aren't going to get to your goal. You might say, "Hey, I'm going up and not down. I'm not stalled out." You may be going up all right, but ultimately you are going in the wrong direction. On the other hand, even more difficult to understand is when you are detoured or downright lost, but in reality you are moving toward what you want in the end.

To discern the proper direction, it is important for us to have a good understanding of the dream. Even people who don't have their dream from God know this principle. If you ever go to a big city, you will often see an area of the city that's surrounded by tall, wood walls. This is an area where major construction is going on, and they often have a big mural or architectural picture of what is being built behind those walls. You'll see a beautiful image of a skyscraper, or apartments, or some other eye-catching structure. But if you peek inside the wooden barrier, it looks like they are going the wrong way. It's a mess! But what you see is not the final product. It is a necessary step to build something truly impressive.

The same is true with our dreams. Sometimes as we pursue our dreams it feels like we are going in the wrong direction. But if we have a good understanding of our dream, we also know there are things that need to be dug out of our lives, instilled in us, or refined in us before that dream can become reality. Remember, the big-picture goal for God is also our character and our relationship with Him.

Overall, God is always moving our dreams forward. However, while He does there might be times when we seem to be going backward instead of forward. Even though our ladder is leaning on the right building, it can seem like we are going down instead of up. It doesn't matter how we feel from time to time, though, because God will help us to reach our goal.

Knowing the end at the beginning reveals whether or not we are going in the right direction and sets us at ease during the sometimes difficult process of reaching out for what we have dreamed.

PRINCIPLE NUMBER FIVE:
Knowing the End Shows You If You Are Really Progressing

Once I was watching a police reality show on television. In the episode I saw a police officer drive up to a residence, where billowing smoke was coming out of the back of the house. He was afraid someone was in trouble and obviously had the desire to save them, so he ran up and pounded on the door. He pounded and pounded, but nobody answered. This really worried him, so he got even more worked up and started smashing windows out of the front of the house with his night stick. By the time he smashed all the windows, an elderly woman came to the door and said, "What is it?"

The officer said, "Get out! Your house is on fire!"

About that time a voice on the radio came on and said, "The fire is next door." It turned out the smoke was coming from the back of the neighbor's house, which was on fire. The city had to buy that elderly lady a lot of new windows!

The policeman's dream to save innocent people who were in danger was a good dream, a noble dream, and an important dream: He worked hard, fervently pounding then smashing away. But the dream contained a fatal flaw. It didn't match up with what was really happening around him. Thus, he didn't get the results he dreamed of.

In a way this principle forms a major part of the story of our faith. The Bible says about Jesus: **The stone which the builders refused is become the head stone of the corner** (Psalm 118:22; see also Matthew 21:42, Mark 12:10, and 1 Peter 2:6). What does this mean? It means Jesus was the answer, the final piece to God's prophetic plan that He had been building for centuries through His people, the Hebrews. Jesus was the key to the whole vision and dream the patriarchs had had from the beginning. Jesus said, **Abraham rejoiced to see my day: and he saw it, and was glad** (John 8:56). By faith Abraham saw the fulfillment of the ages.

How did Jesus become **the stone which the builders refused?** Quite simply, the Jews had lost touch with the dream. God had made His dream for all His people clear—He had revealed the end from the beginning—but they had lost sight of it. They had their noses in their scrolls day and night, busy studying about the Messiah, but when the Messiah showed up they crucified Him. They didn't realize how far God's plan had progressed, and when He appeared right in front of them, they couldn't recognize Him.

Do you see the importance of holding onto your dream and checking and evaluating where you stand in relation to it? Knowing the end at the beginning makes clear whether you are just busy or really progressing toward your goal.

PRINCIPLE NUMBER SIX:
Knowing the End Reflects the Biblical Dynamic of Creation

Any building you see was created twice. It was created first in an architect's office, through imagination, computer programs, engineering calculations, and on paper. Then people took those plans and the appropriate materials and brought into being what was on those blueprints. The whole thing is a process. First the plan will go to local authorities, who will say, "Okay. We see it. We see the dream and approve." But what they see is just an expression of the dream—not its final fulfillment.

So it is with our dream. In a way, everything has two creations. The dream is the first creation—the sense of where we are going and knowing the end at the beginning. Then we walk it out, and that expression—the outward, observable, touchable, tangible expression of that dream—is the second creation. The point is, you can't have the second creation without the first creation.

Did you ever notice in the book of Exodus, from chapters 25-30, God told Moses what the Tabernacle would look like. He showed him every single detail, down to metals, measurements, types of cloth, and ingredients. The vision was very exact. At the beginning of chapter 31, God anointed two men—Bezazel and Oholiab—with creative power to put it all together. And when you keep reading, you get it all over again!

At the end of Exodus 35 you again read about how anointed Bezazel and Oholiab were. Then you get a blow by blow description in chapters 36-39 of how they created everything you had read about previously, according to the vision Moses had from God at the beginning. Obviously, these articles are very important, but these chapters also demonstrate the two stages we are talking about here: Creation by vision, then creation in the natural realm. God has ordained them both, one after the other in a certain order, as the way His will manifests in the Earth.

Knowing the end at the beginning reflects the biblical principle of the two creations of our God-given dream, which is first seen in the spirit realm and then manifested in the natural realm.

PRINCIPLE NUMBER SEVEN:
Knowing the End Gives You a Reason to Rejoice When the Dream Is Fulfilled

Recently we dedicated what we call our "180 Building," which was a dream come true. It was a God-given dream to have a wonderful, incredible facility for our teenagers. We conceived the dream, we worked and gave toward the dream, we prayed and waited on the dream, and then the dream was a reality. When it finally was built, do you know what we did? We went over there as a church body and had a sort of open house to tour the facility and show off all the neat stuff it had. We rejoiced and celebrated because we knew we were seeing the full manifestation of our dream and the final, outward expression of our vision.

When they brought back the Ark of the Covenant to Jerusalem after years of delay, David was so excited about that dream coming to pass that he danced until his clothes fell off (2 Samuel 6:14)! His celebration embarrassed his wife, but he was so caught up in it all that he considered what he did totally appropriate. Celebration is the right thing to do when a dream God gives you comes to pass. Knowing the end at the beginning reveals the moment we are to rejoice and honor God, thanking Him for a dream fulfilled.

Father, dream Your dreams through us. You know we don't mean some New Age silliness. We're asking You to stir in our hearts Your purpose, Your divine destiny, and the way You want to use us. Show us how to be blessed and to be a blessing through Your dream. And Lord, show us the end at the beginning. We need to see the end with clarity. Give us Your strength to run with patience the race that is set before us, looking unto Jesus, who is the author and finisher of our dreams. Help us to pattern our race after Him, having a joy set before us. Keep us focused on that joy, so that we can endure the cross we must bear and despise the shame, withstanding the contradiction of sinners, along with all the hassles and challenges and disappointments that hit us along the way. We know You will make them just fall away from us because we keep Your dream in focus, always looking unto You. In Jesus' name we pray. Amen.

DOES YOUR DREAM EXCITE
YOU OR TERRIFY YOU?

When we talk about the dreams of God in our lives, we use great characters from the Bible as models and templates for what to do and what not to do. In this discussion, eventually we are going to turn to how they reacted to the dream when it first came to them, and it occurs to me that virtually every single person in the Bible is a regular person like you and me. At the end of the day they are just normal folks. This is important to realize before we discuss their responses to God's dream for their lives because it is so easy to think they are different from us and therefore more worthy.

The truth is, nobody is worthy without Jesus, and everyone is made worthy only through His shed blood. When it comes to dreams, God does not give them because of our own efforts, our charisma, or our virtue, but rather because He has laid claim to us in Jesus. We are sanctified in Him through Christ, and although we are weak in our natural selves, we are strong in Him. His power and grace working on our behalf puts us in a position of humility and awe. Every believer falls into a humble posture of personal powerlessness when they come into contact with God Almighty and His purposes for them.

That said, we need to consider how it is for us when God imparts a dream. We are going to feel some things! Ideally, we have recognized our powerlessness and are in awe of God because we know we are just plain vanilla, but we have also engaged the vision and are in tune with Him. Whether it is in business, ministry, marriage, or community, we say, "This is what God has for me. This is my calling and place in the world. I see it, I can envision it, and I am dreaming it. God is showing me the end here at the beginning."

After God gives us a dream and truly births it in our heart and mind, the reality of it starts to hit us and our emotions react. Why? We have already established that—we are human! When it comes down to it, we generally react one of two ways. We either get really pumped up or scared out of our wits.

The first way we might react is like Moses did when God called him. God said, "Moses, I'm giving you a dream. It's a dream of deliverance for My people. I have heard their cry, Moses, and I have seen their plight and the injustice of their circumstances. I'm going to move on their behalf, deliver them, and take them out of Egyptian slavery. I'm going to bring them out of bondage to their very own land, a land flowing with milk and honey. I'm going to restore that which the canker worm, and the palmer worm, and the caterpillar, and the locust have devoured in their life, because I'm a God of restoration. I'm going to do something wonderful. I'm about to move, Moses."

Moses was very excited. He said, "Oh yes, Lord! Amen! Let it be!"

Then God broke the news to him. "Moses, you are the one I've chosen to do this. You're going to spearhead the whole thing and lead them out."

What did Moses say? "I can't do it, Lord! Get someone else."

That's one possible response when God gives us a dream—fear, trepidation, and terror.

The other possible response is pretty consistent with the mindset of a seventeen year-old.

"Joseph, I'm going to make you a great leader."

"Oh, man, bring it on, Lord! I'm ready. I know I can do that. I can do it right now, God! In fact, let me go tell my brothers about the whole deal this minute!"

You know what happened after that. What made both Moses' response and Joseph's response inappropriate was

MAKING YOUR DREAMS A REALITY

that neither fully grasped the weight of the divine dream. God needed to do a work in both of them. He needed time for them to realize how His dream would work in their lives. They had to see that He was the author, the finisher, and the power behind the dream—not them.

How does God do that work? In Acts 1:4, before Jesus ascended into Heaven, He commanded His disciples, "Now wait here in Jerusalem, and don't leave until I send the Holy Spirit." First Corinthians 15:6 says Jesus appeared to five hundred people, but Acts 1:15 says only one hundred twenty were in the Upper Room when the Holy Spirit fell. Even then Jesus couldn't get everyone to show up for church! But all those who did were filled with the Holy Spirit and spoke in other tongues. When they went into the street, some people of the city gathered around and said, "These people are drunk."

That's when Peter lifted up his voice and said, **For these are not drunken, as ye suppose, seeing it is but the third hour of the day. But this is that which was spoken by the prophet Joel; And it shall come to pass in the last days, saith God, I will pour out of my Spirit upon all flesh: and your sons and your daughters shall prophesy, and your young men shall see visions, and your old men shall dream dreams** (Acts 2:15-17).

Please notice Peter did not say and Joel did not prophesy, "When I pour out my Spirit on all flesh, you are going to run around the building like a wild person." He didn't say, "When I pour out my Spirit on all flesh you are going to be offensive to people. You will have spiritual pride because you are full of the Holy Ghost."

No, Peter said what Joel had said, "This is exactly what was spoken by the prophet Joel. God said He would pour out His Spirit on all flesh, and we would have visions, dreams, and prophesy to one another." This also means we would be better able to see the dreams for our lives.

One of the real earmarks of a Spirit-filled believer is having a better comprehension of God's dream for their life. This is what I believe was a major aspect of what Joel was talking about. Understanding from the Spirit helps us to temper out the excitement and the fear of God's dreams in our lives so we can move forward as He would have us to move forward.

I want you to keep this in mind as I discuss some reasons why your dream might excite you on the one hand and terrify you on the other. First, let's look at four fears your dream might cause you.

REASON FOR FEAR NUMBER ONE:
Fear of Failure

This is one of the strongest reasons we resist a major dream or challenge. We say, "If I try it and it doesn't work, what will happen? What will people think? I tried to do something for God before, and it didn't work out. I don't want to fail again. I don't want to go through that again." Because of emotional thoughts like this, all connected to a fear of failure, we are terrified by the dream we received from the Lord.

This was Moses' situation. He was concerned about who was going to believe him, how well he could speak, and how strong a leader he was. He also remembered how his people had gotten angry with him for killing an Egyptian soldier (Exodus 2:11-14). He didn't exactly leave town a hero! That is why he started to make excuses that he couldn't do what God wanted him to do. He was terrified of the dream God was casting in front of him. Moses was obviously plagued by the fear of failure.

This kind of fear has to do with putting your eggs in the wrong basket. If God gives you a dream and you are terrified by it, you have to place that dream in His hands instead of your hands. You have to remember that He is the author and finisher of this dream, not you.

The same is true of the opposite reaction, by the way. Let's say you are excited like Joseph and say, "I have got a dream! Bow down to me because I'm going to be great leader." That overconfidence is just as dangerous as the fear of failure. The only remedy is to place your dream squarely in God's hands.

To be free of the fear of failure and have a godly confidence, you must lay down the dream and completely immerse yourself in God.

REASON FOR FEAR NUMBER TWO:
Fear of Success

There are people who get on the verge of something great, of great success, and will sabotage themselves to wreck the whole thing. There can be many reasons for this, and most of the time it is some kind of fear issue. Maybe it is because they have never felt worthy to succeed. Maybe their mom or dad said they would never amount to anything, that they could never be great. Perhaps it is the fear of the unknown—new demands they know would be placed on them if they rose to a new level of success and achievement. Whatever the reason, God wants them to get past their fear and press into His plan for them.

The Bible has multiple examples of people who "shot themselves in the foot," seemingly for no reason. King Saul was afraid of the people, so he made an illegal sacrifice and lost God's anointing to be king as a result (1 Samuel 13:6-14). David's son Amnon was first in line to be king, and what did he do? He gave in to his lust for his half-sister Tamar, raped her, and then spurned her! As a result, Tamar's brother Absalom murdered Amnon. Absalom didn't do any better than Amnon, however. After murdering Amnon, he overthrew his father David and ran him out of Jerusalem. In the end David's general, Joab, killed Absalom, which restored David to the throne. (See 2 Samuel 13,15,18.) Either one of these guys could have been the next king of Israel.

Judas could have repented like Peter (they both betrayed Jesus), but instead he gave in to fear and condemnation and hung himself (Matthew 27:3-5). He forfeited being part of the greatest movement the world has ever seen. And then there was Adam, who gave up more than anyone. He was about to live forever in Paradise when he seriously sabotaged himself (and his wife and those of us who were to follow) by eating the forbidden fruit (Genesis 3).

It seems there is a human trait to be self-destructive when we get spooked, and many times even the thought of greatness can cause us to run for the hills in terror. Therefore, we need to place all our trust in God and move on with His courage. His ability working in us is the remedy for any fear of success we experience.

REASON FOR FEAR NUMBER THREE:
Fear of Being Unprepared

David consecrated himself in Psalm 31:15 when he prayed, **My times are in thy hand.** David knew that only God knows when we are ready for whatever He has planned for us. There are times when we cry, "I'm ready!" and He knows we really aren't. There are also times when we cry, "I'm not ready!" and He knows we really are. That's when He'll nudge us and tell us it is time to jump out of the plane.

The fear of not being ready will cause us to procrastinate or not even start moving on the dream God has given us. If we get started, it can keep us from advancing from one stage of fulfillment to the next. That's why this fear needs to be dealt with.

We have a positive example in young Solomon in 1 Kings 3:5-12. After his father David's death, God appeared to him in a literal dream and spoke to him about his kingdom. Solomon answered, "I'm not ready. The job is too big for me." But Solomon did not give in to his fear. We read on to see that he chose to lean on God to get past that fear. His fear of his own inexperience was real, especially since he was so young, but his trust in God was more powerful. When he asked God for wisdom, his request revealed he was more ready for the job than he thought.

We face the fear of being unprepared the same way Solomon did. We rely completely on the Lord and His wisdom and strength to take the steps He is asking us to take in realizing our dreams.

REASON FOR FEAR NUMBER FOUR:
Fear of Man

Sometimes when we apprehend something great for ourselves, we shrink back from it because we worry about what others might think. We wonder if they might say something like, "Who do you think you are?" We are paralyzed by the fear of what others might think and say in response to our dream.

A prime example of this was Gideon. In Judges 6 the angel of the Lord appeared to him and commanded him to destroy his father's altar to Baal. Gideon actually obeyed, but he did it in the dark and hid after he did it! He was afraid of how the people would react. As it turned out he was right—the people were not very happy with him. But his mistake was hiding the vision because God was in it and saw him through.

Another example is Saul. God ordained him to be king of Israel, but when the call became public, he hid among the saddle bags and they had to dig him out (1 Samuel 10:22-23)! Humility is a virtue, but we shouldn't run from the plan of God for our lives, nor should we be frightened of people's opinions. Proverbs 29:25 says, **The fear of man bringeth a snare: but whoso putteth his trust in the Lord shall be safe.** It is important to believe God's Word and be fearless, even as we recognize that not everyone is going to be happy about our dream.

Now let's look at how your dream can excite you.

Excitement Number One:
No More Limits on God

If you have a dream from God, you will be able to invest yourself and give yourself more fully to Him than you may have ever done before. Why is that? Your dream involves a revelation of God Himself. Moses and Joseph didn't just get a vision from God, they both discovered the heart of God to deliver His people. And once they saw God for who He was, the sky was the limit.

A real heavenly dream does the same thing for you. It takes the limits off how you perceive God. He becomes bigger, better, more loving, more powerful, and more interested in you and those you love than ever before.

When the Israelites came out of Egypt, they did not see God for who He really was. In a way this was natural, since they had been in slavery for generations. God used Moses to do signs and wonders to correct their understanding of Him, but first He had to get the blinders off Moses. He did this through miracles like the burning bush and the rod of authority and power. By the time Moses led the Israelites out of Egypt, they had witnessed supernatural signs, plagues, and being miraculously delivered out of slavery in Egypt.

To top it all off, when Pharaoh pursued them and it looked like they were trapped at the Red Sea, God parted it and delivered them again. That was not only salvation for the moment, it was a three-dimensional vision of who God was, an understanding of His grace and love for them that was meant to carry them for generations. That event is celebrated today in the Jewish Passover because it is such an enduring heavenly drama about who God is in relation to them as a nation.

God's dream in us can destroy all limits you have placed on His grace and love toward you, which is why the dream should excite you. It should overwhelm you with a deeper understanding of who God is. It is good to be a faithful church member, and there is virtue in consistently showing up week after week. But God wants more than just religious habits out of you. He wants you to see more than the inside of a church. He wants you to see Him, and that happens as you dream and let Him dream through you. When that happens—when God totally invades and infuses you with His purposes—you get excited about Him along with your dream.

EXCITEMENT NUMBER TWO:
No More Limits on You

This is a critical point. You might say, "God is an awesome God. He's a great God. He's a mighty God. He's all-powerful, all-knowing, and present everywhere by His Spirit. Hallelujah!" You believe that, but do you personalize it when it comes to seeing a dream through? In other words, in general you say, "He's awesome in me, for me, and through me," but when you get a dream that comes from Heaven you say, "I'm not good enough, smart enough, or strong enough to do this."

Getting a dream from God forces you to remove the blinders and see yourself through His eyes. You begin to understand that the truth about what God can do in you, for you, and through you—that you can be awesome like Him—is real. In your own mind and strength you are very little, but in Him you are great.

When David received the word of the Lord that his kingdom would last forever, he went into the sanctuary of the tabernacle, sat down, and prayed, "Who am I to you, God? Is this the way you usually deal with mortals—telling them their dynasty will last forever and ever?" (2 Samuel 7:16-19, my paraphrase). David caught a glimpse of himself in God's eyes, and he saw that in God there were no limits imposed on what his life could be. In the same way, your dream takes the limits off you. His power and character become personal and reside in you as divine potential.

EXCITEMENT NUMBER THREE:
You Think You Can Do It

There are also some negative, incorrect, and ill-founded reasons for excitement over a vision. One wrong reason for excitement is simply that you think you can do it like you could do any other task in your life. In other words, you might see it as a challenge, but you still have a natural confidence. Just as dangerous as being terrified you can't do it is falling into the trap of believing you can do it in your own mind and strength.

As I have pointed out, this was the case with Joseph. He got all excited about being king of the world and boss over his brothers from the dream he had. But time and experience knocked that natural confidence out of him. He learned the hard way that it was God's vision and dream working in him and through him. He could not view God's dream lightly, like it was just another task for the "Wonder Kid."

You might be a highly motivated person. You might be gifted and bright and have the Midas touch. Whatever you do succeeds. If you are like this, then I congratulate you for the great gifts God has given you. But let me also warn you that a dream from God is radioactive. It is like something from another world—because it is. You are in for a humbling experience if you think you can do it in your spare time, or just by using the same tactics and life strategies you have used with other achievements. You need God to do it in you and through you.

EXCITEMENT NUMBER FOUR:
The Hope of Impressing Others

The last emotional reaction I want to address is that of excitement over the prospect of looking good to other people. This is a natural reaction in a world that is so focused on how others see us. It is the flip side of being afraid people will think we are being presumptuous or silly. It is what happens if we begin to really pay attention to the thoughts that say, *Wow! My boss/parents/friends/neighbors will be blown away when they see me doing this.*

We see this even in ministry. "Won't people think I'm wonderful if I get my ordination card? I can just hear them say, 'You're ordained?' and I'll say, 'Why yes, I am.' Their eyes will get really big and they'll say, 'Wow, when did that happen?' and I'll just answer nonchalantly, 'Oh, it is just something I've been doing on the side.' At last they will admit, 'That's really impressive!' and I'll say, 'Oh, stop!' like it was nothing.

Unfortunately, even believers like to look good to other people, and some will use the sacred call of God to do it. Jesus addressed this with His disciples. **And he came to Capernaum: and being in the house he asked them,**

What was it that ye disputed among yourselves by the way? But they held their peace: for by the way they had disputed among themselves, who should be the greatest (Mark 9:33-34). Like everyone else, the disciples had the vision, the dream, and the call of being close to Jesus all wrong. It wasn't about being looking good or having a great reputation. It was about serving others. That is true greatness.

Paul said something similar concerning how he viewed his life. **Circumcised the eighth day, of the stock of Israel, of the tribe of Benjamin, an Hebrew of the Hebrews; as touching the law, a Pharisee; Concerning zeal, persecuting the church; touching the righteousness which is in the law, blameless. But what things were gain to me, those I counted loss for Christ. Yea doubtless, and I count all things but loss for the excellency of the knowledge of Christ Jesus my Lord: for whom I have suffered the loss of all things, and do count them but dung, that I may win Christ** (Philippians 3:5-8).

Looking good to others had ceased having any appeal for Paul because he had encountered Jesus on the road to Damascus. Jesus trumped everything else. Excitement over divine reality had permanently overtaken excitement over personal reputation. This conviction enabled Paul to press through to see his God-given dream fulfilled.

HAVING THE COURAGE TO BE EMOTIONALLY STABLE

I want to conclude this chapter with a story. One time I invited some of my board members to go to Tulsa with me to investigate some ministry opportunities. While we were there, I wanted to show them some of the different ministries in Tulsa, and I made arrangements to go up to Oral Roberts' office. He wasn't going to be in town then, but I said, "Let's just go. I want you to see Brother Roberts' office." I had contacted his secretary, who had worked for him for over fifty years, and she had made the arrangements.

We went to the top of the Learning Resource Center and stepped out of the elevator into this magnificent office. Stacks of prayer requests, banded together in bunches so Brother Roberts could easily pray over them, covered the room. There were thousands of them stacked on every credenza and desk and table.

What was most amazing was the sweet presence of God in that place. We stood there, taking in the peaceful, serene, anointed atmosphere. Personally, I was just in awe and reverence of this great man of God. He is a great man and a great leader. To be in his office where he did his work was just tremendous.

I looked down, and on his desk I saw a wooden plaque that said, "Make no little plans here." Those words really impacted me, because they gave me a glimpse into the heart and mind of a great man who had dreamed some big dreams and done some great things. In that context, I just knew he had had his moments of terror and excitement, but he also had learned to overcome the highs and lows by keeping his eyes on God.

I encourage you to let God stir in you, refine in you, and develop in you a wonderful dream for every aspect of your existence. That might take time, but at least open your heart to allow Him to speak to you and show you what He wants for your life. Then, whether you become excited or terrified, keep your eyes on Jesus! If He is the author of it, He will be the finisher of it. You can rest from either being overly excited or horribly afraid because you know He is going to work in you, through you, and for you.

Father, we thank You for Your Word. We purpose to let You give us our dreams, which include our hopes, aspirations, and goals. We praise You whether we respond to our dream with great excitement or terror. You are the God of the dream in our heart. Help us to fix our eyes on You, to trust in You, and to rest in You alone. In Jesus' name we pray. Amen.

DYING TO OUR OWN ABILITIES

THE SUBJECT OF THIS CHAPTER relates closely to the subject of the last chapter. I say this because if you compare your dream with your own abilities and capacities, you will naturally respond, "I cannot do that" (the beginning of a terrified reaction). In that assessment you are both right and wrong. And if you compare your dream against your giftings and strengths, your response will tend to be, "Sure, I can do that" (the basis for excitement). That reaction also is both right and wrong.

To handle our reaction to our dream in a right way, a godly way, we must die to ourselves and our own abilities. Now Word of Faith people in particular don't like the word death. I'm not crazy about the idea of death either, but the part of us that wants to respond to God's dream by assessing our own abilities to accomplish it has to be put on the altar.

Here is the point of this chapter. We must say, "Lord, it doesn't matter if I think I can, and it doesn't matter if I think I can't, I lay that at your feet. Work in me, grace me, change me, and prepare me, so that I can do what You have called me to do in Your power, and not in my own strength."

In John 12:24, Jesus says, **Verily, verily, I say unto you, Except a corn of wheat fall into the ground and die, it abideth alone: but if it die, it bringeth forth much fruit.** THE MESSAGE Bible translates this verse, **Listen carefully: Unless a grain of wheat is buried in the ground, dead to the world, it is never anymore than a grain of wheat. But if it is buried, it sprouts and reproduces itself many times over.**

Do you have the picture now? We have to lay our assessment of our abilities at the Lord's feet. We must let them die so that His miraculous, resurrection life can spring forth in our lives, reproduce itself, and be fruitful.

In 2 Corinthians 5:15-17 (brackets mine) the apostle Paul said, **And that he [Jesus] died for all, that they which live should not henceforth live unto themselves, but unto him which died for them, and rose again. Wherefore henceforth know we no man after the flesh: yea, though we have known Christ after the flesh, yet now henceforth know we him no more. Therefore if any man be in Christ, he is a new creature: old things are passed away; behold, all things are become new.**

Jesus died for us and rose from the dead so we could have a new life in Him. We are not to live unto ourselves, for ourselves, or by ourselves. That's what Paul means by "after the flesh"—in the natural way instead of the spiritual. We are called to live unto Him. Although we know about ourselves and about others after the flesh, and we even know about Jesus after the flesh, as believers we are not to know anyone after the flesh. We don't want to evaluate ourselves and others—and especially not the Lord Jesus—from a fleshly, carnal, natural perspective.

For example, if I call my wife "God's gift to my life," "my helpmeet, "my partner," "my cheerleader," and so forth—no matter what things look like in our marriage at that time—I'm seeing and knowing her from a spiritual perspective. But if I call my wife "the old lady," or "the old ball and chain," I am cheating myself! I am viewing her and knowing her after the flesh instead of after the Spirit.

If we simply accept the way we know ourselves naturally or after the flesh and declare, "Well, that's just the way I am. You know I have always been that way, so I guess that's just the way I'm always going to be"— we are doing ourselves a world of harm because we are stuck in our own natural abilities. We must see ourselves as more than natural human beings. We are new spiritual creatures in Christ. We have His nature and walk in His abilities.

Paul said, "We don't want to know anyone after the flesh. In fact, we don't even want to know Jesus after the flesh anymore." Jesus taught and performed a few miracles in His home town, but the people got upset about it. They said, **Is not this the carpenter, the son of Mary, the brother of James, and Joses, and of Juda, and Simon? and are not his sisters here with us? And they were offended at him** (Mark 6:3). They were offended at Him simply because they knew Him after the flesh. They didn't know Him after the Spirit.

There was Jesus, preaching these astonishing messages, signs and wonders following His ministry, and people were focused on knowing Him after the flesh! "Hey, wait a minute, who does He think He is? I mean, Harriet, that's the guy that built our kitchen table, and He's a miracle worker? Yeah, right."

In Mark 6:4 Jesus said, **A prophet is not without honour, but in his own country, and among his own kin, and in his own house.** He couldn't do much of anything because these people had watched Him grow up. He was just the carpenter's kid. His disciples could have made the same mistake and focused on natural things. I'm sure they could have said, "We remember when we walked all day and even Jesus was so tired, He wanted to go to bed before the six o'clock news!"

My point is that if we can make the conscious choice between knowing people after the flesh or appreciating who they are in God, then we can make that decision about how we see ourselves as well. We don't want to know Jesus after the flesh, we sure don't want to know others after the flesh, and we also don't want to know ourselves after the flesh. Most of us are very aware of our human frailties and shortcomings, but we have to look beyond these weaknesses and see who we really are in God. We are new creatures in Christ, and all those old things are passed away.

"Oh, I have always done this."

Old things are passed away.

"I have always had a tendency to..."

Old things are passed away.

"I have always thought that..."

Old things are passed away, and all things are become new.

First Corinthians 2:9-11 says, **Eye hath not seen, nor ear heard, neither have entered into the heart of man, the things which God hath prepared for them that love him. But God hath revealed them unto us by his Spirit: for the Spirit searcheth all things, yea, the deep things of God. For what man knoweth the things of a man, save the spirit of man which is in him? even so the things of God knoweth no man, but the Spirit of God.**

Whatever you would dream for yourself, God wants to do something exceedingly, abundantly, tremendously higher and greater than anything you would ever dream up yourself. And the key to understanding the full height and depth of these verses is knowing these things come only by the Spirit of God. It is not a natural thing!

Verse 12 of the same passage says, **Now we have received, not the spirit of the world, but the spirit which is of God; that we might know the things that are freely given to us of God.** God wants us to get connected with Him spiritually, to be in tune with Him spiritually, and to perceive spiritually—all because He wants to reveal to us the things He wants to freely give us.

Then verses 13-16 continue, **Which things also we speak, not in the words which man's wisdom teacheth, but which the Holy Ghost teacheth; comparing spiritual things with spiritual. But the natural man receiveth not the things of the Spirit of God: for they are foolishness unto him: neither can he know them, because they are spiritually discerned. But he that is spiritual judgeth all things, yet he himself is judged of no man. For who hath known the mind of the Lord, that he may instruct him? but we have the mind of Christ.**

Have you ever tried to explain spiritual truths like salvation, healing, or tithing to people who aren't saved? "Well, it works like this. I give ten percent of my income to

God, and then I do better, I'm more successful, and I have more than...."

"Oh, sure you do. You give it to *God*. Right."

As believers even we cannot understand spiritual things with our natural minds. We must train our minds to think and to see things like Jesus sees them—spiritually. Paul went on to tell the Corinthians that their carnal thinking had caused divisions and contentions among them because they were forming factions under Apollos and himself. But these men happened to have a harmonious relationship.

Paul said, **Who then is Paul, and who is Apollos, but ministers by whom ye believed, even as the Lord gave to every man? I have planted, Apollos watered; but God gave the increase. Now he that planteth and he that watereth are one....: For we are labourers together with God.** (1 Corinthians 3:5-6,8-9).

What does this mean? To go to the next stage in developing and embracing God's dream for us, we have to ask God to give us a dream. Then we have to make certain it is a God dream and not a Jeff dream or a Nancy dream. Once we have articulated that dream and have a clear picture of it in our heart and mind, and once we see ourselves painted into that picture, then we have to come to grips with our own natural tendency to size ourselves up and see if we are equal to the task. That automatic self-assessment needs to die and to be buried.

If I were to ask someone a question as simple as, "Could you be an usher in the church?" many (thinking of their own abilities) would respond with, "An usher? Well, sure. Of course I could be an usher. I could start right now if you want me to. I can pass the offering bucket, pat people on the back, and greet folks. Sure I could be an usher."

That kind of attitude needs to die. Being an usher in the church may seem a light task, but it is not. The ushers are responsible to help foster an environment and create an atmosphere in which God can speak to people, in which they can worship and praise without interruption, and where order reigns as a reflection of God's nature. There's a whole lot more to ushering than just passing a bucket.

The "Yeah, sure, I can handle that," thinking has to die. We need to say about even those things as simple as ushering, "Lord, I'm going to let that attitude die, and I ask You to bring forth in me a total reliance on Your strength and discernment. I want to bury any self-reliance and independence, and I want new life in You to spring forth with a greater understanding of my purpose, my ministry, and my calling. Show me, Lord, how much I need Your grace, Your wisdom, and the gifts of the Spirit."

I'll give a perfect example of what I mean. Once Oral Roberts preached at our church, and in the service was a wild-eyed, difficult young man. We tried to minister to him, but he kept disrupting the service. Finally, the ushers had to help him out of the service to maintain order. A few months later when I was at the sheriff's department working some hours as a chaplain, I glanced at the photos on the wall. They were pictures of criminals they were looking for, and among them was this young man's photo. He was wanted for homicide!

I said, "I know that fellow."

The deputy on duty said, "You do?"

I said, "Yeah, he goes to my church."

They said, "Well, if he shows up again, just call us and say, 'This would be a great day for you to come to church!'"

An usher who is in tune to the mind of the Spirit would discern this young man, but an usher who is there just to pass the bucket would probably not discern anything. With Spirit-led ushers, a situation like we faced with that troubled young man can be dealt with the way God wants it dealt with. We might not get it right every time, but we would be more prepared to handle it by knowing people by the Spirit.

What follows is a list of five simple principles for letting our own assessment of our abilities die (with the terror or the excitement of our God-given dream), so that God can bring about something greater than we could in our own mind and strength.

PRINCIPLE NUMBER ONE:
Discouragement Often Comes Through Someone Close to You

One of the most important principles to grasp when it comes to dealing with a vision you have received from God is that the favorite entry point of discouragement is often through someone close to you. If you tell your dream to someone you don't know or is not that important in your life and they reject it, the impact is limited. They might say, "That's the most ridiculous thing I ever heard in my life." But since you are not deeply connected with them and don't necessarily value their opinion, you generally have the ability to not be bothered by what they say.

It is a different story when it comes to what your spouse, family, close friends, and sometimes your boss, co-worker, or pastor think. They can push your buttons! That can be painful because they are close to you and/or you care about what they think. Their negative words just naturally get under your skin. In other words, it is fleshly.

What angers us and pushes our buttons is that these people know our flesh, and we know their flesh. This intimacy can cause them to make immediate, natural evaluations of what we say and do if they don't know better. They know us best, and we trust them the most, so they can encourage us more than anyone else when they are in the Spirit. But their words can do a lot of damage if they are thinking in the flesh. One way or another, we react more strongly to those who are close to us.

Young David was anointed to be king over Israel by the prophet Samuel right in front of his older brothers (1 Samuel 16:13). When he took some lunch to them at the battlefield, his elder brother Eliab chewed him out and called him conceited because he challenged the men of Israel to fight Goliath (1 Samuel 17:17-29). Eliab had a problem with David, probably because he figured he should have been chosen to be the next king. Still, David said, "What's your problem? Why don't we kill this giant?" He shook off the discouragement, but it certainly was something he had to deal with.

In John 7 Jesus' own brothers were sarcastically encouraging him to become a public figure because they didn't believe in Him. He dealt with them in a different way than He dealt with the Pharisees who openly and viciously persecuted Him. After all, they were His half-brothers and were dear to Him.

As a pastor and counselor, there have been people in whom I have invested myself and poured my life, my time, my money, my prayers, and my love. Then one day they just said, "We're outta here," and took off. This can be devastating from a natural perspective if I take it to heart and get discouraged, wondering what I might have done wrong.

I think about my dream to move my church forward and reach the world, and the wondering starts again. *If I can't keep a family in whom I have invested so much, how in the world do I ever think I'm going to reach the world and build His church?* That's when I must allow God to change my perspective and say, "Wait a minute! Jesus said, 'I will build My church' (Matthew 16:18), and that means I'm not called to build His church."

I just took my eyes off the hurt and disappointment people have caused me in the natural and returned to what God's Word says. I'm back on track and seeing things His way. I'm also back on my way towards fulfilling my dream, because it isn't my abilities but God's abilities that will make it happen. I did not allow the hurt from those close to me to cloud my vision of the truth that it is God's ability and charisma that will drive the dream and see it through.

God wants us to be aware that discouragement is sharpest when it comes through those we love. This doesn't mean they are bad for us or for the vision. It just means they count the most and know us best, and their words and actions weigh on us more than other folks' words and actions. We are to love and appreciate them, but we live our lives according to God's will and dream for our lives.

PRINCIPLE NUMBER TWO:
Never Surrender Your Dream to Noisy Negatives

First Kings 19 relates the story of Elijah and the voice of God. Elijah had just destroyed the prophets of Baal in a display of the power of God. He had seen fire fall from Heaven. He had restored Israel's faith in the One True God. The deaths of the prophets of Baal had purified the land. Then Jezebel threatened to kill him, and this great man of God got scared to death and ran for his life.

Elijah eventually stopped running to rest for awhile. He proceeded to fast for forty days as he made his way to a cave on Mount Sinai. Elijah then complained to God, and God told him to go outside. When he got to the mouth of the cave, he heard and saw some dramatic natural disasters: a tempest, an earthquake, and a fire. But God was not in these things. Finally, Elijah heard a whisper, and he heard the voice and the dream of God for his life from that point forward.

The lesson we learn from this story is that Elijah, in spite of being God's man, had surrendered to fear. The loudness of the visions he saw from the mouth of the cave reflected all the inner "noise" he was listening to—his success against the prophets of Baal, Jezebel's threats, and his failures and limitations. Things were so bad he actually asked God to take his life.

God wanted him to turn off the "noisy negatives" and to hear His soft voice of reason and truth. That's how your dream comes, and that's how your dream is sustained. It is not by high drama and flashiness but by quietly listening with ears to hear God's direction for each step of your life.

PRINCIPLE NUMBER THREE:
Your Dream Is Spiritually Discerned

It is important not to evaluate your dream in terms of your natural abilities because God is going to ask you to do something that is beyond you. If you try to perceive it naturally, knowing yourself and others after the flesh, you will probably be frustrated. You must have a spiritual point of view when it comes to your dream.

Consider Joseph, the adoptive father of Jesus in the New Testament. He was engaged to a godly young girl named Mary, and one day she said to him, "Hey Joseph, guess what? The angel Gabriel appeared to me and told me I was going to give birth to the Son of God, who would be Savior of the whole world. When I asked how (since you and I have never been together), he said the Holy Spirit would take care of that. He did, so I thought you should know that I am with child by the Holy Spirit."

However big your faith is, that is quite a lot to swallow. Joseph was a good guy and a great man of God, but the vision was just too spiritual for him. Like everyone else (especially engaged young men), he was conditioned to consider these issues after the flesh and the natural mind. And given the magnitude of the issue, I think most would agree it shouldn't be held against him that he needed some help!

Knowing all this, God sent an angel to Joseph in a dream, just like the Joseph in Genesis. The angel told him not to be afraid, that Mary was really carrying the Son of God. This dream enabled Joseph to perceive his situation spiritually, to see it through God's eyes. It also empowered him to carry it out in terms of God's thinking and abilities instead of his own thinking and abilities. Joseph received the word of the Lord and the manner in which God communicated that word. Then he was free to pursue the dream because he had broken out of his natural way of thinking into God's spiritual way of thinking.

Peace is the key to spiritual discernment because God communicates on the wavelength of peace. If you want to listen to AM talk radio but tune the radio to FM, you will be frustrated because you are on the wrong wavelength. The sooner you get on the right wavelength, the sooner you will hear what you need or desire to hear. In the same way, God's dreams are spiritually discerned on His wavelength of peace. So cultivate God's peace and spiritual discernment will follow.

PRINCIPLE NUMBER FOUR:

See Yourself by the Spirit Not the Flesh

When I say you must change the way you see yourself, to see yourself with spiritual eyes instead of natural ones, it is really liberating. The reason it sets you free is because you can be your own worst enemy, an expert at making excuses for yourself that really serve to hinder you.

We all say things like, "Well, you know, I just wasn't raised to think that way, so I guess I'm just sort of stuck," or "I'm not going to be able to do that because I come from a very poor family," or even "I grew up in a wealthy family, and I'm just not used to being with those sort of 'down and out' people." Our list of excuses goes on and on. We are black or white or red. We are too old or too young. We are too educated or not educated enough. This is seeing ourselves according to the flesh not the Spirit.

Look at Gideon in Judges 6. He hid in the winepress and tried to save a little food for his family from the marauding enemies of Israel. Then the angel of the Lord showed up and said in verse 12 (my paraphrase), "The Lord is with you, valiant warrior."

Gideon basically looked around and said, "Who, me? I'm the littlest guy from the littlest tribe in the nation. We are constantly getting beaten up by the bad guys, and you are calling me a mighty warrior? What gives?" But the Lord was speaking to him in pure spiritual realities. He saw Gideon after the Spirit, while Gideon was still stuck in his own excuses that sprang from seeing himself after the flesh.

God wasn't leading Gideon on or giving Him a motivational pep talk. He spoke in spiritual language based on spiritual perception. He saw Gideon for who he was in the Spirit. Gideon, on the other hand, was not even remotely close to that. All he could see were his troubles and his limitations. He had not died to his own self-assessments. And he was a worse enemy to himself than the Midianites he was hiding from.

You can be the same way. Your perspective of yourself has to die and be buried, so that God can raise you up to a new place in Him. He wants all of your excuses—who you are and are not, what you can do and can't do—to be replaced by His view of you. This doesn't mean you throw all reason out the window or that you cannot celebrate your natural abilities and gifts in a healthy way. It just means that when it comes to the dream and its fulfillment, God's view of you rules.

PRINCIPLE NUMBER FIVE:
Recognize That the Dream Itself Does Not Die

We must be willing to allow our assessment of our abilities to die so that a new life can spring forth by the power of God's Spirit in us. At the same time, we have to recognize that while our self-perception goes through a painful process of death and rebirth, our dream remains alive and even becomes stronger. It may feel like it dies at times, because our emotions can be confusing. But the real death is going on in the realm of our flesh and our natural view of things not in the dream, which is of the Spirit.

A great example of this is found in the story of David and the Ark of the Covenant in 1 Chronicles 13. When he first became king, he decided he wanted to bring the Ark from the little town where it was stored after its return from exile in Philistia. This was a great dream of restoration for the nation of Israel. David consulted with the elders and they agreed, so he loaded the Ark on a cart, formed a parade, and started toward the city.

As they proceeded toward Jerusalem the oxen stumbled, and when a guard named Uzzah steadied the Ark so it wouldn't fall, the wrath of God struck him down. David got so scared he stopped everything, cancelled his plans, and left the Ark in the house of Obed-Edom instead of continuing the journey. Three months later David heard that Obed-Edom was getting blessed like crazy, so he went back and brought the Ark all the way to Jerusalem.

What do we learn from this? David erred twice. First, he didn't consult with God about moving the Ark. He just consulted with the elders. As I have said, advice is good but not when you leave God out! Second, David leaned on his own understanding about transporting the Ark. He was supposed to have the Levites carry it on poles, but he used a cart instead. The result was that an innocent man died, and David's excitement died.

David thought the dream of restoring the Ark to its place was dead, but when he saw how blessed the man who kept the Ark was, he realized the dream was really of God and was still alive. It may have seemed like it was all over when Uzzah was struck down and the parade came to a screeching halt, but in reality all that died was David's reliance on his own thinking and abilities. He got over his, "Oh yeah, I'm the king and God's anointed and I can do anything" attitude, and humbled himself.

In 1 Chronicles 15:2 it says David made sure the Levites carried the Ark when he brought it from Obed-Edom to Jerusalem. David learned to get past the confusion that comes in the emotion of the moment. He discovered that the death of relying on his own reasoning did not mean the death of his dream. In fact, it gave it more life!

We need to learn the same thing. When we are personally going through the throws of death regarding the assessment of our abilities, we need to realize that in the end our flesh passes away like chaff, but the plan from God is eternal.

Father, each of us has a purpose. You didn't create any accidents, and You didn't put us in the body of Christ for no reason. We all have a mission and a purpose. You have a destiny carved out for every one of us, which You impart to our hearts and minds as a dream. We want to embrace Your dream, and we want to know the dream is significant and has many roles in our lives. But Father, when we think about that dream, we tend to respond in the flesh with excitement or fear because we are made of dust. Help us to die to those things so You can do the greater work in us that only You can do. We pray this in Jesus' name. Amen.

Your Dream Alone Will Not Get You To Your Goal

WE HAVE DISCOVERED A LOT about dreaming. We saw how important it is to yield to God's dream for us, and we have talked about posturing ourselves properly so we move towards that dream within God's will and by God's power instead of our own. Now we will discuss a truth that many have missed to their own great loss.

I have learned that the dream alone won't get you where God wants you to go. There are people who have had dreams tucked away in their hearts and lived their whole lives never doing anything with their dreams. Their dreams were powerful and had great potential, but something didn't connect and they never became a reality. So we have to ask, "Lord, what is that connection that will make our dreams a reality?"

Hebrews 3:16-18 says, **For some, when they had heard, did provoke: howbeit not all that came out of Egypt by Moses. But with whom was he grieved forty years? was it not with them that had sinned, whose carcases fell in the wilderness? And to whom sware he that they should not enter into his rest, but to them that believed not?**

The children of Israel had a dream God had given them, the dream of entering a land flowing with milk and honey, which was their inheritance as children of Abraham. But not all of them gave themselves completely to that dream. Some **believed not,** and the dream did not benefit them. It did not come to pass for them.

The Promised Land was God's dream for Israel and part of His larger purpose for humanity. But the older generation didn't participate because they didn't believe. Again, God gave them the dream. He gave them a promise and a firm hope of a desired end, but they did not have faith in His dream or His promise. That's why Hebrews 3:19 says, **So we see that they could not enter in because of unbelief.**

We do not want to repeat their error, and God speaks directly to the church in Hebrews 4:1, **Let us therefore....** In other words, let's bring this message home for today. This happened a long time ago, but the experience of Israel must be applied to us in our world, our life, our ministry, our family, and our church. The Bible says, **Let us therefore fear, lest, a promise being left us of entering into his rest,** any of you should seem to come short of it.

God doesn't want us to fall short, and He's not threatening that. He is just saying we need to take care so we do not repeat the mistakes and errors of history. He says in Hebrews 4:2, **For unto us was the gospel preached, as well as unto them: but the word preached did not profit them, not being mixed with faith in them that heard it.**

The dream of going into the Promised Land was God's will. He gave them His word and His promise that it was theirs. Why didn't it profit them? If it was His will, why didn't He just pick them up and carry them into the Land? Because He gives people free moral agency, the ability to choose, and the Israelites chose not to believe His word or His promise. The Word that was preached to them—the dream and the vision God cast before them through Moses—**did not profit them, not being mixed with faith in them that heard it.**

Faith is a choice we make. When we choose to mix faith in God with the dream, the word, and the promise He has given us, it will profit us. Faith is the connection! Faith brings the dream from revelation to manifestation, from an idea to reality. Hebrews 4:3 completes the thought with, **For we which have believed do enter into rest, as he said, As I have sworn in my wrath, if they shall enter into my rest: although the works were finished from the foundation of the world.**

If God has given you a dream, in His mind it is a completed deal. All the provision you need, all the anointing you need, all the people you need, all the buildings you need, all the airplane tickets you need—they are all included in His plan from the foundation of the world. However, although it is accomplished in the spirit realm and in the mind of God, your dream won't become reality, profit you, or bless others if you don't mix the dream with faith.

Following are five keys to help you keep from being fooled into thinking that the dream alone can get the job done. You must have faith in God and believe His promises to you to see it happen.

KEY NUMBER ONE:
Mixing Your Dream With Faith

How do you mix your dream with faith? If you know how God wants to use you—through a dream and a sense of destiny or purpose—you have to go to God's Word. Find out what God says in His written Word about you, your dream, and your situation. The Word is the first step because **faith cometh by hearing, and hearing by the word of God** (Romans 10:17). Consulting the Word will edify you and build your faith so you will harmonize your vision with the perfect will of God.

When God gives you your dream, it is a natural tendency to say things like, "I don't know how this is going to work," or, "Who, me?" or even, "Fat chance!" But those words do not conform to what the Bible declares about you. Your mind might be fighting the dream because it is so overwhelming in the natural, but in your heart and with your mouth you need to declare the truth. "I can do all things through Christ who strengthens me. My God will supply all my need according to His riches in glory. I can run through a troop and leap over a wall. Greater is He that is in me than he that is in the world. And if God be for me, who can be against me?" (See Philippians 4:13,19; Psalm 18:29, 1 John 4:4, and Romans 8:31.)

Once you begin to mix faith with your dream, you will surprise yourself! You'll be running around, telling people things like, "I'll tell you one thing, Brother and Sister, I know you have doubts, but I believe and have faith I'm going to do great things for God!" You need to get a little bit sassy not towards God but in God and in His ability.

When the twelve spies Moses sent into the Promised Land came back, two of them mixed the report with faith, and ten of them mixed it with fear. Mixing it with fear cost many lives. They and all who agreed with them died in the wilderness without ever receiving God's promise. But Joshua and Caleb, who mixed the dream with faith, were the only two of millions who came out of Egyptian slavery into the Promised Land. Because they stood on God's Word, believed His promise, and mixed faith with the dream; they were the only two from the older generation to enter God's rest with the younger generation, who were born during the forty years in the wilderness.

KEY NUMBER TWO:
A Dream Mixed with Faith Is a Restful Place

When you begin to mix faith with your dream it won't be a place of anxiety, fear, or worry. The passage you just read from Hebrews 3 says you enter a resting place in God by having faith in Him. James 1:5-6 confirms this with, **If any of you lack wisdom, let him ask of God, that giveth to all men liberally, and upbraideth not; and it shall be given him. But let him ask in faith, nothing wavering. For he that wavereth is like a wave of the sea driven with the wind and tossed.** God is not angry if you ask for wisdom to work out the dream. All He asks for is faith, that you believe Him.

This passage encourages us to strengthen our faith. Then, when we ask God for something, we will have the confidence in His goodness, faithfulness, and integrity to ask without wavering. There are whole denominations whose message is, "Well, you never know what God will do." Well, I know what God will do! He will do what He said He would do in His Word. We must never drift into doubt and unbelief.

We don't understand every life experience, but that's not the issue here. The issue is resting in God, knowing He is faithful and true. We need to ask in faith and not waver, knowing He is good, He is for us, He's thinking good things about us, and He always has our best interest at heart. This confidence has a specific effect upon us. We rest in God when we have faith in Him. We are not tossed about by fear and doubt.

There are people who have a dream, but their faith in God wavers. Their doubt works its way out in their lives through a driven, self-centered attitude that says, "I have got to get ahead, work more hours, and make this happen!" They are not resting in God. They are not at peace. They are workaholics and driven maniacs.

Driven people can be preachers, business people, or even stay-at-home parents. The issue isn't what you do or your title but an inner posture toward God that is off base. Folks who are driven are tossed and always moving about—even in church. You see them at a couple of services, and a year or two later you see them again. When you ask, "Where have you been?" they reply, "The Lord has just led me everywhere." They are tossed around, and they coat it with all kinds of nonsensical spiritual language. This is a sure sign they have never mixed their dream with faith because mixing faith with a dream brings rest and stability. When you are really anchored in your faith in God, you will not be driven or tossed around. You will live in His rest.

KEY NUMBER THREE:
Faith Without Works Is Dead

We are asked in James 2:14, **What doth it profit, my brethren, though a man say he hath faith, and have not works? can faith save him?** God is not talking about the dream or its desired end and goal. He is talking about actively participating in the dream He has for us. The verse defines works as a corresponding activity and consequence of faith.

The question, **can faith save him?** balances the truth of Ephesians 2:10, **For by grace are ye saved through faith; and that not of yourselves: it is the gift of God: Not of works, lest any man should boast.** We understand God's grace saves us through faith—the connection between the idea of salvation and the reality of salvation. But let me tell you, if you are truly living a life of faith, it will result in activity. And the Bible says your saving faith will cause you to act in faith.

What doth it profit, my brethren, though a man say he hath faith, and have not works? can faith save him? If a brother or sister be naked, and destitute of daily food, And one of you say unto them, Depart in peace, be ye warmed and filled; notwithstanding ye give them not those

things which are needful to the body; what doth it profit?
(James 2:14-16).

James draws a parallel between faith and works.
Someone is hungry and you pat them on the back and say,
"Well, be filled now." Then you walk away and do nothing. Where's the beef?!! You talk faith but you do not act
in faith. You have to have action to back the sentiment and
the vision of seeing them filled. Go get them a cheese-
burger, or if they are a vegetarian give them a tofu burger!

James says in verse 17, **Even so faith, if it hath not
works, is dead, being alone.** If you have faith without
some corresponding activity, your faith is dead. That is a
strong statement! He goes on to say, **Yea, a man may say,
Thou hast faith, and I have works: shew me thy faith
without thy works, and I will shew thee my faith by my
works. Thou believest that there is one God; thou doest
well: the devils also believe, and tremble. But wilt thou
know, O vain man, that faith without works is dead? Was
not Abraham our father justified by works, when he had
offered Isaac his son upon the altar? Seest thou how faith
wrought with his works, and by works was faith made perfect?** (James 2:18-22).

How this works in your vision and dream is going to
depend on the dream God gives, on you, and on your circumstances. I cannot sit here and tell you what action to
take. But I can tell you that you will need to move on your

dream in a concrete way. David had a dream of building a temple for the Lord. In 2 Samuel 7:1-17 God sent Nathan the prophet to tell him, "Good thinking, but no. You're a man of war, and it isn't your vision to carry out. Your son, on the other hand, will be a man of peace, and he will build the temple."

What did David do? He submitted fully to the word of the Lord, and then he went as far as it allowed him to go. He accumulated enormous amounts of material and wealth for the building of the temple. He did all he could humanly think to do within the guidelines the Lord had given him.

We need to have that attitude. Faith in God is more than just choosing to believe. It is a love for Him that moves us. We need to trust and then move like David did. As our faith is accompanied by action, God will bless our dream and bring it to pass.

KEY NUMBER FOUR:
Faith and Works Together Are Greater

There is another truth found in James 2:22, which says, **Seest thou how faith wrought with his works.** The Greek word translated "wrought" is *sunergeo*, which means "to work together with someone, cooperate."[1]

---

[1] Spiros Zodhiates, *The Complete Word Study Dictionary: New Testament*, (Chattanooga, TN: AMG Publishers, 1992), p. 1341.

From it we derive the word "synergy," which is defined as, "The interaction of two or more agents or forces so that their combined effect is greater than the sum of their individual effects."[2] In other words, when certain elements are brought together they amount to more than they did apart (either in substance or effect)—sort of a 2+2=5 thing.

An illustration that will give you a clear picture of faith and works together is to give strands of thread to hundreds of people in a room. At any time anyone could tear apart their little piece of thread without any problem. But through synergy—all those strands being woven together to form a rope—it would be much harder to break it. The parts work together to achieve something greater and stronger.

Faith and works must be together, working synergistically. It is the combination of the two that manifests the power of God in our lives. James points out that Abraham took God's dream for his life and acted on it without faith when he had a son with Hagar instead of Sarah his wife. The result was Ishmael—a wild man who was the father of the Arab nations (Genesis 16:4,11-12). Not all but most Arabs have always hated Israel and many today cause tremendous problems throughout the world.

Don't be like Abraham! Stay in faith. Dream your dream, mix it with faith, let your actions be in step with

---

[2] http://www.thefreedictionary.com/synergy

how you believe, and the result will be blessing—both for you and for those who will receive from your dream.

KEY NUMBER FIVE:
Dream Maintenance Is Important

Paul said to Timothy, "Don't neglect the dream!" This is my paraphrase of, **Neglect not the gift that is in thee, which was given thee by prophecy, with the laying on of the hands of the presbytery. Meditate upon these things; give thyself wholly to them; that thy profiting may appear to all** (1 Timothy 4:14-15). In other words, "Timothy, you have a dream, you have a call, and you have gifts. But you have to work with them and cultivate them."

Only you can maintain your dream. When I say "maintain" the dream, I mean to mediate upon it, to revisit the place where you received it, and to keep it real and fresh and powerful in your mind and heart. Don't just dream it, frame it, put it on your wall, and never look at it again. Do what you need to do to move your dream forward and make it a reality. Stay focused.

Discouragement is part of living in this world and can rob you of your focus. You can talk "victory, victory, victory" all the time, but if you don't have something in your spiritual arsenal to combat discouragement, you are not going to stay focused and continue to move forward. You are not strategizing for dream realization. Wise dreamers understand they need to build themselves up in their dream along the way.

We have talked about Elijah. In 1 Kings 18 he scored a mighty victory for God against Baal worship. He called fire from Heaven. He killed the wicked prophets of Baal. It was all part of his dream and vision for a pure Israel—an Israel that didn't waver between two opinions but worshipped God only. But after that victory Elijah crashed. At one threat from Jezebel, he ran for his life. Soon he was saying he had had enough and wanted to die. Elijah needed some maintenance—a spiritual tune-up!

Consequently, God sent him on a journey of forty days and nights to Mount Sinai, where Moses received the Law. It was the perfect place to revisit his dream for Israel. Here is where God dealt with Elijah, and in spite of all his complaints gave him new marching orders and a word of encouragement—"I have seven thousand who haven't bowed the knee to Baal" (1 Kings 19:18, my paraphrase). The dream had not died because the Giver of the dream had not become discouraged. It was Elijah who had worn thin to the point that he just wanted to give up the ghost. He needed to go back, revisit and renew the dream, and do some dream maintenance.

As a result of his lack of faith, of allowing discouragement to overtake him, Elijah's mantle soon was passed to Elisha, and Elisha was mightier than Elijah. So I strongly urge you not to neglect maintenance! Stay in the Word, pray in the Spirit, stay focused on your dream, mix it with faith, and you will see great things come to pass.

Lord Jesus, help us to dream mighty, heavenly dreams and mix them with great, unwavering faith. Help us to rest in Your promises, knowing You are faithful and have our best interest at heart. Give us wisdom and inner strength to act in faith and to maintain our dreams. Help us to follow the examples of those in Your Word who teach us with their lives how to connect faith to our dreams and move forward to see our dreams become reality. In Your name we pray. Amen.

PERSIST IN PURSUING YOUR DREAM

HOW DO YOU PERSIST IN PURSUING your dream despite setbacks, disappointments, and sometimes tragedy? You know your dream won't be fulfilled in your life all by itself. It must be mixed with faith and maintained in faith. But what do you do when you encounter the obstacles, and challenges, and sorrows that come from living in a fallen and imperfect world? These are the things that conspire to hinder, stop, and destroy the dream God has given you.

Galatians 6:9 says this: **And let us not be weary in well doing: for in due season we shall reap, if we faint not.** That verse is your answer! God is wise and merciful, and he knows that as life-giving, dream-fulfilling, and-God pleasing it is to "do well," this world has a way of wearing you down. You can become tired of doing the right thing— even the thing that can fulfill the dream you want more than anything else.

You can have the noblest and highest dreams a person can dream for every area of your life. You can dream dreams for your kids. I'm not talking about oppressively imposing your will on them, but believing your kids will be blessed, have confidence in themselves, and be productive members of church and society. You also can have dreams for business, for ministry, or for any number of worthy things God would bless. Whatever the dream is, when you begin to grasp that dream, I promise you there will be opportunity to get weary! Discouragement will try to invade your soul and steal your peace. That's why God assures you in His Word that if you refuse to get weary and continue to do well, if you draw on His strength and not faint, in the end you will reap. You will see your dreams fulfilled.

I have to be honest with you, there have been areas in my life where I have given up too quickly, gotten weary in well doing, and thrown in the towel. I'm not saying this has happened in every area of my life, but I'm sure there have been things God dreamed for me that I forfeited because I said, "That's just too much hassle." So I want to talk to you about persistence in pursuing your dream, regardless of setbacks and circumstances. I have broken down this vital information into seven points, which I call points for persistent pursuit.

POINT ONE: TIME DELAYS

Once again Joseph is a perfect example of this principle. He was a seventeen-year-old young man who was ready to roll. He had had a powerful dream, he was ready to rule and reign, but it took thirteen years to see it come about. That's a long time! It is what we call a real time delay.

When our church moved into its present building, I told my wife Melissa, "This building is not the sanctuary. This building is a classroom building for our children's ministry, and I'm not going to act like we are going to be in here very long." I said that because at the time, with about a hundred people, it was a step of faith to do this. But we knew God was going to bring more people, and we built it in faith.

I made up my mind and understood things a certain way. I said, "We are going to be in this building just a few months, and then we are going to start building the sanctuary. Therefore, since we are not going to be here very long, it would be a waste of money to build a platform. Just slap down a few tiles. That'll be fine for the time being."

That was fifteen years ago.

Time delays are just part of pursuing dreams, and they are what they are. They can't give you an excuse to say, "Well, you know, we could probably make it another twenty years in this building, since we've been here so long." No, that's giving into the discouragement that comes with a time delay in a different way. In our case, it would be selfish and short-sighted because to grow is both a gift and a command of God.

Thank God Joseph never said, "Well, this is taking too long, so I guess I'll just accept being in prison for the rest of my life. I'm successful enough without those crazy dreams I had as a kid. I'll just be satisfied with where I am." That would have been a disaster for Joseph, for Egypt, and for his entire family. The same is true for us. People get blessed as the church grows and expands. This dream is from God, and real vision from God usually comes with delays.

Be ready for time delays, and don't allow them to discourage you or to stop you from moving forward in your dream.

POINT TWO: PERSONNEL CHANGES

Sometimes we think we have figured out how God is going to bring our dream to pass and with whom we will walk it out, then changes happen. There could be a change of those who fight the battle with us in prayer. We could change a business partner, a mentor, a pastor, neighbors— I can't begin to mention all the possibilities. There is always a possibility for change in the people who have a major role in the fulfillment of your dream.

In Acts 15 Paul and Barnabas were traveling together, realizing their dream of bringing the gospel to the Gentiles. They were about to embark on a new journey when Barnabas said to Paul, "I want to take my cousin John Mark along." John Mark had traveled with them before, but he had gotten homesick and left the merry missionary band just when things started getting interesting and they needed his help (Acts 13:13). Paul remembered this and said, "I don't want him to go with us because the last time he was with us he acted like a little sissy and had to go home."

Barnabas was really set on taking John Mark, and neither he nor Paul would budge. In the end the two great apostles parted company over it. Barnabas went one way with John Mark, and Paul took Silas and went another direction. They were still carrying out their ministry dream, but there was a change in personnel.

Paul had learned from Barnabas, and Barnabas had learned from Paul. Theirs was a reciprocal relationship that bore fruit for the kingdom, and it seemed they would always travel together—but they didn't. Although later their relationship was restored, the change in personnel continued.

What you must remember is that even when feelings get hurt and the nature of your relationships change, it doesn't cancel out the dream. A change in personnel never changes your calling, your ministry, or the promises God has given you.

POINT THREE: METAMORPHOSIS

Metamorphosis simply means a gradual change. This is important to you and your dream because sometimes the form of your dream "morphs" into something that looks different (sometimes very different) than what you envisioned at the beginning. The essence of it is the same, but it looks different than you thought it might when you first dreamed it.

I'm not a geneticist by any means, but I understand two words from that field of study. The first term I want to point out is "genotype," and the second term is "phenotype." Genotype simply means the genetic predisposition to look a certain way. You've got a genetic predisposition to be tall or short, have dark hair or light hair, a certain eye color, and so on. That's your genotype, and everyone has one. Phenotype, on the other hand, is the actual manifestation of the genotype. If we took a snapshot of you today, the phenotype is exactly what you look like.

The phenotype of your dream—the actual manifestation—might actually come out differently based on the genotype. The genetics of it are what are really important, because that's what the pure essence or purpose of God is. This is just a little illustration of a spiritual truth from science. It works because, as Romans 1:20 tells us, all creation bears witness to the absolute truths and ultimate power of God.

Our dreams can come out differently in their outward manifestation than we imagined they would when they first formed in our spirit. Hero after hero in the Bible experienced this. David was an old man when Bathsheba pleaded for her life and the life of Solomon. Another son of David's had staged a coup and had taken power. So David intervened and placed Solomon—not his firstborn son or even the next in the royal line—on the throne in a counter coup. And he probably wondered how things had developed the way they had. In Solomon, all God's promises to him came to pass, but the Kingdom of Israel looked different than he had envisioned when God had given him those promises.

Peter must have stood in wonder in Cornelius' house, with all those Gentiles speaking in tongues before he even gave the altar call. He had something else in mind when he got the Great Commission from Jesus! But God knows what we don't know. He will see the dream through if we are faithful, even though the dream doesn't look exactly like we thought it would look.

I like to joke with Melissa that I'm sure she had a dream about who her husband would be, an ideal man in her imagination. And the poor thing—bless her heart—she got me! She's told me I look a little different than she anticipated, but she loves me and I love her. The genotype of the dream held true even if the phenotype wasn't what she thought it might be!

Sometimes you have preconceived ideas. The dream is right, but when you finally get there, it is not exactly what you thought it would be. In spite of all of that, you have to stick with the dream. Don't be discouraged when it changes a little bit. You need to say, "Well, this is what God has done, and I accept what it is." It's not about disappointment. It is about outward change, and you need to be ready for it.

POINT FOUR: BAD REPORTS ALONG THE WAY

Along the way you are certain to run into some discouraging news. Some of this bad news might come from nay-sayers, some of it might be genuine challenges that you have to deal with, and some of it might constitute things you really don't have to be concerned about. Whatever the source, bad news has a way of coming. The best way to handle it is to take it as part of the process and deal with it as the Holy Spirit leads you.

In Numbers 13 Moses sent twelve spies into the Promised Land. Out of twelve men, only two came back with anything good to say. In spite of God's promise that He had already given the children of Israel the Promised Land, despite all the miracles He had done for them, the other ten spies were nay-sayers. "We're like little grasshoppers, and they are all giants."

This kind of bad report will derail a dream quickly if you let it, and the entire nation of Israel did just that. The result was that the dream died for millions of people. They died in the desert and never saw a single grape from that land except what the spies had brought out. The trick here is that the report was solid and well-founded. All the spies were of high reputation, or they wouldn't have been chosen. They were brave and smart, the "James Bond 007's" of the Hebrews! They had seen giants first-hand. Why not believe them? Because what they said was against the word of the Lord. Their report was an evil report because it stood in opposition to God's dream for them.

Similarly, we have to be careful of circumstances and reports that are bad news. The Bible says in Psalm 112:7, **He shall not be afraid of evil tidings: his heart is fixed, trusting in the Lord.** This describes a believer whose dreams are grounded in God, who won't be shaken no matter what happens or what news comes. They realize there are always going to be reports that tell them the dream is not going to become a reality. They choose to persist and pursue it regardless of negative talk or bad reports.

POINT FIVE: OTHERS MAY TRY TO BLOCK YOUR GOALS

This is a difficult point to address not because it is complicated but because it can be one of the toughest to deal with. It can be incredibly frustrating and difficult. On the one hand the Bible says we do not battle with flesh and blood (Ephesians 6:12). That is pure spiritual truth, and it sounds so good and right in our prayer closet. But when we are dealing with a person or a group of people who are really causing us trouble, it can get under our skin until we feel like lashing out at them.

At times like these you have to remember the battle is with evil spiritual forces. This is tough to handle when a real person is looking you in the eye and doing something that is directly hindering the dream you received from God. But you are being challenged to go from the milk of the Word to the meat of the Word, to act like an adult in the Lord instead of a baby. Spiritual meat is not a hidden mystery of the Bible. It is maturity in action.

I am going to be transparent and share some of my testimony about our church's building projects. When we started building we were in the County of Riverside. Upon going to the county for the planning meetings, in the process of developing our land, we found out we were in the sphere of influence of the city of Rancho Mirage. Therefore, they had input at the hearings. They said hateful things about us, announcing they didn't want a church and using every excuse in the book to hinder us. We had proposed a two-story building on our land on Bob Hope Drive. They said, "We don't want two-story buildings.

There are no two-story buildings out there."

I said, "Well now, right across the street there are some homes, and I have been up on the second story of those homes myself. I've personally looked out the windows on the second floor of those two-story homes."

"Well... there's just a bedroom up there," they said, and I would get so angry. It preaches real fine to talk about what I said and should have said, but those folks were not church folks. I saw them as the enemy who was standing in our way.

Then things got worse. We were annexed into the city of Rancho Mirage and had to deal directly with them. I was a pastor, a man of God, and I was passionate about my dream of a community of faith. We wanted to build buildings, touch kids' lives, and bring people to Jesus. As I passionately presented our vision, the city planner I talked to yawned and then went on and on about forms, fees, and red tape. I had showed up with briefcases stuffed with all that nonsense, but I was still so frustrated.

All I wanted to do was build something for God and His people, but I was getting nothing but opposition. I confess I got so frustrated I would just see stars and be fuming mad. Finally I said, "Lord, I'm just going to claim favor with the Planning Commission."

Looking back on it now, I see how God helped us to keep our dream moving forward by leading me to do two things. First; we prayed for favor and for the City Council. As a result, we really have had favor with them. Imagine that. Prayer works! But it is spiritual meat, real maturity, when you are cheated, lied about, and treated downright mean and ugly for no reason—and you just keep loving, blessing, and forgiving. Why? Because that is how mature Christians act. It is our job description.

Second, I had the good sense to send someone else to those planning meetings! I sent someone who knew how to handle the paperwork, the details, and all the ins and outs of that sort of thing. That way I could pray better because I wasn't in constant conflict with folks who didn't understand the walk of faith.

When other people show up and try to hinder or stop the vision God has given you, pray for favor and pray for them. I promise you, not only will the situation turn around, but you will grow into a whole new level of spiritual maturity.

POINT SIX: LIMITATION COLLISIONS

When you are dreaming your dream and beginning to walk things out, you will run into your own limitations. After I had pastored my church for about ten years, one day I was in prayer. I was enjoying His presence, having a quiet time of being still and knowing He was God. Suddenly I just said, "Lord, I have taken this church as far as

I can; I don't know what I'm doing anymore."

I had attended a little Bible college, and they had just taught us to preach the Word. They didn't teach us about church government, structure, finance, or working as a team. They said, "Just preach the Word." Certainly preaching the Word is the core of ministry, but you also need to know other things to have a successful church. I realized I needed more. I said, "Lord, I'm either going to turn this church over to someone who knows what they are doing, or I need to find out myself how to do it."

I made the decision to go back to school, and I looked for an accredited institution that offered the subjects I needed to do what I was called to do. For my situation, that meant going to a local community college in my thirties, sitting there with a bunch of eighteen-year-old kids. They had those little school desks, and I didn't fit in them, so I sat in the back in a chair. It was humbling, but I managed to finish my bachelor's degree.

Then I found out about a program at Oral Roberts University where working clergy could get their master's and doctorate degrees. I flew to Tulsa one week a month for about six years. I did a lot on campus—not by extension—flying back and forth and working like crazy. It involved tremendous effort, but in the end I had a master's degree and a doctorate degree.

The point is not that I have nice looking diplomas hanging on my wall to impress people who get impressed by that sort of thing. The point is that I made a decision to enter into a difficult but necessary process that could take me beyond the limitations I had run into, limitations that were hindering my dream. I wanted to build a great church that grew and was healthy and functioned the way God intended. That's a great vision—some might say *the vision*. But what I had learned at Bible college was just not enough to get the job done.

During my time at ORU, into my doctorate, I heard the former dean of the ORU School of Business say to a bunch of high-profile pastors, leaders of thousands of people, "If you guys are making more than four or five decisions a year, you are not very good delegators." That was me. I didn't understand about team ministry, and I found that instead of facilitating growth and empowering others, I was actually clogging the flow of the ministry because every decision had to pass by my desk. This brother mentioned four or five decisions a year, and I was making four or five decisions an hour. I realized I had been clueless.

My dissertation was on strategic planning. I didn't choose that subject as some sort of abstract, academic exercise. I did it because it had to do with my weakness, where I needed to grow and become strengthened to realize my dream. You may not be required to get a master's or doctorate, but I can tell you that realizing a dream means looking at yourself very hard from time to time, discovering where you come up short, and then doing something to bring you up to speed.

The Bible is a veritable catalog of folks who looked at their dream, looked at themselves, and realized they were ignorant and unqualified. That's where God comes in. Thank God, He doesn't leave us to ourselves!

One way or another, by His grace and some good, old-fashioned hard work, your shortcomings will be overcome if you are not afraid or too proud to evaluate yourself, and then are willing to let God give you what you need to succeed.

POINT SEVEN: LOOKING BACK CAN BE EASIER THAN MOVING AHEAD

We read in Galatians 6:9, **And let us not be weary in well doing: for in due season we shall reap, if we faint not.** Sometimes looking back is easier than moving forward. When God delivered His people out of Egypt and moved them toward the Promised Land, they ended up in the wilderness for a long time. Exodus 17 tells us they complained to Moses every time they encountered the slightest problem or challenge.

They said, "Moses, did you bring us out here to kill us? Did you bring our children and livestock out here to let them die of thirst? Are we never going to eat meat again? What is the plan, man?" Numbers 11 records other complaints, which were basically whining, "We want to go back to Egypt, because at least in Egypt we had leeks and onions, water, and meat to eat." They listed all the things they had experienced through sensory knowledge in Egypt. In other words, it was all material stuff.

The children of Israel were so stuck in their past they never really dove in head first and completely lost themselves in the dream God had for them. They'd never smelled, tasted, or seen themselves living in the land of milk and honey. They had never laid hold of the Promised Land by faith. It had never become substance or evidence (Hebrews 11:1) to them because they kept looking back to Egypt, saying, "Oh, let's go back to the familiar. Let's go back to a place we know how to deal with. Even though it was a painful place, at least we knew what to expect." It always seems much easier to go back to what's familiar rather than to go forward into the unknown.

I used to be a maniac about coffee. I'm a one-cup-a-day person now. I have moderated my life and have more self-control, but back in the day one of my priorities in prayer was getting Starbucks in Palm Springs. Finally they opened a store downtown, and I happily drove the ten miles to get there. One day I stood in line with about forty people. We were lined up out to the street, waiting to pay three bucks for a cup of coffee.

I was having a lot of fun with this guy in front of me. I said, "Can you believe we are in this line, just waiting to pay three bucks for a cup of coffee? The product itself can't cost them more than twenty cents, and the cup probably costs more than the coffee! What do you say? You think the place is going to make it?" We laughed, but then I had a shocking thought. My coffee connoisseur brain popped up with, *You could have had Folgers back at the office.*

This may be a silly example, but the point is that human beings are often tempted to take the path of least resistance. At that moment, going back to drinking Folgers at the office represented the familiar path I had walked in my past. But by their very nature dreams are forward things. We have to resist the comfort and temptation of the familiar and be willing to forge ahead into new, uncharted territory—which may cost us something.

Consider Noah. When he was five hundred years old God told him it was going to rain and rain until it became a flood. Noah needed to build something to rescue his entire family and two of every kind of animal on the Earth. So Noah obeyed and began to build the ark according to God's specifications. It took him and his three sons one hundred years to build this boat, which was 450 feet long, 75 feet wide, and 45 feet high. That's almost a million and a half cubic feet, roughly the capacity of 522 railroad cars. Now, that's a big boat!

Can you imagine such a project today, with modern building equipment? Back then, they did it all by hand! Plus, it had never rained before. They had no idea what a flood was. And the concept of the end of life as they knew it sounded as nutty then as it would sound to a secular person on the street today. But it was a good thing Noah trusted God and moved forward instead of living in the comfort of his past.

Following God often means we pursue big dreams that seem humanly impossible and require us to do things that everybody we know thinks are just insane. That's when we are so tempted to look back on how wonderful things were before God gave us this crazy dream. But we must move forward. We don't have to complete the journey today. We just have to take the first steps. Pick up the first board, drive the first nail, and trust God for the rest.

Father, help us to dream Your dream for our lives and not look back, to move forward and not be weary in well doing. Give us Your courage and wisdom deal with time delays, personnel changes, changes in the way our dreams look, bad reports, people the enemy sends to hinder or block our dreams, our own limitations, and the temptation to stay in the comfort of our past instead of forging into our future. You said and we believe that in due season we will reap if we don't faint. Help us to persist in pursuing what You have put in our hearts, by Your strength and not our own. In Jesus' name we pray. Amen.

The Power Twins
of Faith and Patience

PREVIOUSLY WE DISCUSSED the synergy between faith and works, how together they accomplish more than either could alone. In this chapter I would like to take that a step farther. Hebrews 6:11-12 says, **And we desire that every one of you do shew the same diligence to the full assurance of hope unto the end: That ye be not slothful, but followers of them who through faith and patience inherit the promises.** The Bible tells us that the synergy of faith and patience, these two virtues working together in your life, will enable you to realize your dream.

The Word goes on to say in verses 13-15, **For when God made promise to Abraham, because he could swear by no greater, he sware by himself, Saying, Surely blessing I will bless thee, and multiplying I will multiply thee. And so, after he had patiently endured, he obtained the prom-**

ise. I love the story of Abraham. James 2:23 says that he was called the friend of God because he believed God's promise to him. Then in Genesis 15:5 God asked him, "Abraham, can you number the stars in the sky?"

Abraham answered, "No."

That's when God gave him five little words, **So shall thy seed be.** Then, in Genesis 22:17 He told Abraham his seed would not only be like the stars in the sky but also the grains of sand on the seashore. Think about that for a minute. Whether it was the stars at night or the sand during the day, Abraham had constant reminders of God's simple but powerful promise, **So shall thy seed be.**

When God first told Abraham and Sarah they would have a son, they laughed. It was probably a "You have got to be kidding me!" laugh. It was a "Did you hear the one about the hundred-year-old man and his ninety-year-old wife having a baby" sort of joke. It was their natural humanity—their limitations—colliding with God's crazy plan, which struck them as funny in a bitter sort of way. They had been disappointed for so long.

Romans 4:18-21 says this about that time in Abraham's life, **Who against hope believed in hope, that he might become the father of many nations, according to that which was spoken, So shall thy seed be. And being not weak in faith, he considered not his own body now dead, when he was about an hundred years old, neither yet the**

deadness of Sarah's womb: He staggered not at the promise of God through unbelief; but was strong in faith, giving glory to God; And being fully persuaded that, what he had promised, he was able also to perform.

How do we know Abraham was strong in faith? He gave glory to God for the promise and didn't consider the natural circumstances, namely the age of his own body and the barrenness of his wife. It's not that these facts didn't cross his mind, or that he didn't have the sense to know what he was up against in the natural. He just **considered not**, deciding his challenges were no problem for God. Instead, he **considered** and focused on what God had said.

In our terms, we would **consider not** what the doctor said, what the attorney said, what the accountant said, what the stock market said, what the newspapers said, or what our neighbors said—but what God said! Focusing on what God said is a fundamental decision we have to make continuously in the pilgrimage to see our dreams fulfilled.

When you combine Abraham's faith with his patience, you have a powerful combination. Some folks think that walking with God means you can pick up the phone and chat with Him anytime you like. There are some people who spout, "God told me this" and "God told me that," as if they are hobnobbing with the neighbor over a fence or something. But if you read Abraham's story carefully, you will see he would have this incredible experience with

God, who would speak to him and promise him all these things, then He would go away. Sometimes He would stay away for years.

In Genesis 15-16, when God promised Abraham a son and Abraham blew it by having Ishmael with Sarah's handmaid Hagar, he was eighty-six years old. In Genesis 17 when God appeared again and made clear the promised son would come through Sarah, Abraham was ninety-nine. There's nothing in the Bible about God saying anything to him between those times.

I'm not saying you will have to wait twenty years at a stretch for the Holy Spirit to speak to you if you are being sensitive to Him and walking in His Word. We are children of the New Covenant and the Spirit lives within us. But I am saying we need to be more reverent about God speaking to us. Like the old-time Pentecostals, we need to understand waiting on God to get His mind and to see Him move in our lives. That's patience, and it is a virtue many have forgotten. Abraham—someone the Bible tells us to imitate—had plenty of it.

This passage in Hebrews says it was the combination of faith and patience that caused Abraham to see the fulfillment of God's promise to him. His dream depended on these power twins. Now I want to share five points to reveal the depth of the power of faith and patience working together in your dream.

Number One

We Need a Definition of Faith

Hebrews 11:1 says, **Now faith is the substance of things hoped for, the evidence of things not seen.** "Well Pastor Jeff," you might say, "I just have a hard time believing what I can't see." Have you ever seen your brain? Yet you believe you have one, right? I don't want to see my brain! I prefer to just believe it is there. And since we are talking about spiritual realities, have you ever seen Heaven? I haven't, but I firmly believe it is there, and I'm looking forward to the day I will stand in that holy place.

Do I have proof of Heaven—evidence of it? Yes! The faith of God in my spirit gives Heaven substance in my heart and mind and presents the evidence that it is real. For unbelievers the reality of Heaven is impossible to comprehend because they don't have the witness of the Holy Spirit and the Living Word of God inside them. But children of God know that Heaven is real. Their faith gives substance and evidence to it. Faith is what God requires of us to see our dreams fulfilled.

We need faith, but our faith has to be accompanied by wisdom. When I was at Rhema Bible Training Center in the late 1970s, there was a lot of talk about the difference between faith and presumption. I learned that faith was based on the will and Word of God as you walked closely with the Lord. On the other hand, presumption was based on your own ideas and thinking. Presumption assumed God would do things He might not do.

For example, we discussed whether or not "Faith people" should have insurance. After all, if we really trusted God to keep us healthy, fireproof, and accident-proof; why would we need insurance? But I learned that although we live by faith and not by sight, always expecting God's best, we aren't ignorant of the devil's devices, other people's evil tendencies, and our own imperfections. Stuff happens, and sometimes you miss it. So it's wise to have insurance, and it doesn't mean you have less faith in God to protect you. This is simply mixing wisdom with faith.

Take into account your personal weaknesses. You can have complete faith in God, but you cannot have complete faith in yourself or the world you live in.

NUMBER TWO
A Sudden Increase in Faith Must Be Coupled with Patience

Many times we experience what can be called a faith surge. We hear a great message, a wonderful passage of Scripture comes alive in us, or we spend a quiet time with God and faith explodes inside us. That excitement is real, but it is a sort of "spike" in our faith. It is not deeply rooted faith. It is just an escalation of faith, a flash of faith, a sudden increase of faith—that must be coupled with patience.

If we are not wise about these "surges," we can move on them too quickly. We must be patient. Since the faith isn't deeply rooted, it can be challenged and damaged easily. We need to mix patience with that surge of faith, allowing time for it to mature in our mind and heart, to become unshakeable faith. Then, when we act we won't blow it.

Abraham was the consummate man of faith, but he wasn't perfect. God told him his children would outnumber the sand and the stars, and they would inherit the whole world (Romans 4:13). God's promise created a great surge of faith but he lacked patience. Instead of waiting on God for the fuller revelation, he forged ahead in his own understanding.

Sarah said, "Here, take my handmaiden Hagar, and maybe we can have a family through her." (Back then, women could count their maids' children by their husbands as their own.) Probably many factors went into Abraham's decision, including his own longing for a son, his wife's nagging, and a pretty Egyptian maid; but the bottom line was that he simply didn't wait on God to come through.

At the end of the day Abraham made things right, but having Ishmael was a permanent problem for him, his descendents, and all people on Earth. We need to learn the lesson and not repeat it. We need to understand that the excitement that comes with newborn faith doesn't always mean we need to rush into anything, especially when it comes to decisions affecting big dreams. We need to allow that faith to grow deep roots and become stabile, which means having patience with God and ourselves.

NUMBER THREE
Faith Must be Deep and Abiding

When trouble comes it is a strong, abiding faith and not just a surge of faith that will carry the day. Deep, lasting faith comes from walking with God over a period of time, seeing His faithfulness and experiencing His consistency work again and again in your life. There is no shortcut to spiritual maturity. It has to be lived daily for years.

When someone has walked with God, prayed consistently, and suffered hard times only to see God is more wonderful and powerful than they had imagined, that person develops and unshakeable faith in Him. It's the kind of faith that is first cousin to patience also learned through years of experience.

Patience isn't just the ability not to lose your temper when someone cuts you off in traffic or to put up with a tedious task for an afternoon. Bible patience is the virtue of perspective, of seeing your life in the big picture. Although things may seem rough or slow at the moment, you know God has you by the hand, your dream is from Him, and you are making progress.

Faith and patience must be held in balance, and as you cultivate them so they work in tandem you will wake up one day and realize, slowly but surely you have been moving forward. Faith without patience lends itself to short sprints, but unshakeable faith and patience with God's perspective will manifest your lifetime dreams.

NUMBER FOUR
Your Mouth is Your Primary Faith Barometer

I was raised in churches where we were taught, "You never know what God might do, so just hope everything works out." Those words still come from the lips of wonderful, sincere, well-meaning folks. However—and I don't want to come across as overly harsh—those words are also going to get them nowhere in a world that is hostile to anyone living by faith and wanting to see a dream come true in their life.

What is your mouth saying? Romans 4:17 tells us we are to speak and act like our Father, who **calleth those things which be not as though they were.** The Bible does not say we call those things that are as though they are not. Some believers have done this by confusing the meaning and message of this verse. If they break their leg they say, "My leg isn't broken," instead of saying, "By the stripes of Jesus my leg is healed." Declaring the leg is not broken is just a lie, but declaring God's promise of healing—**by** whose stripes ye were healed (1 Peter 2:24)—is speaking the truth of God's Word.

We used to have a little upright model piano in our church, and I had the congregation stretch their hands toward it and say, "Piano, be grand." It sounds comical, but in the humor was a serious spiritual truth. We were calling those things which be not as though they were. However, we didn't say, "You're not an upright piano. You're a grand piano." Faith isn't pretending you don't have a problem or a need. Faith is facing and handling those problems according to the truth of God's Word.

Let's be real, Abraham and Sarah couldn't have babies. He was old enough to be a great-great grandpa, and she was right behind him. This predicament is the context for the verse in Romans 4:17—calling things that are not as though they were. Abraham had a promise and a dream from God of a natural heir, and that's what came out of his mouth. He gave glory to God and said to everyone he met, "Hi! I'm Abraham, the father of many nations." His confession of faith connected to the dream, and Isaac was conceived!

Check up on your mouth. James 1:2-4 says, **My brethren, count it all joy when ye fall into divers temptations; Knowing this, that the trying of your faith worketh patience. But let patience have her perfect work, that ye may be perfect and entire, wanting nothing.** You might say,

"Now Pastor, how can I count it joy when I'm having all these hassles from the devil?"

Jesus endured the Cross for the joy set before Him. He counted it joy. You can draw on His strength to count your troubles joy knowing that as your faith is tried you will become more patient, and then patience will work in you a satisfaction and general contentment with life so that you will lack nothing. Is it fun to count it all joy during hard times? No, it may not be fun, but it is extremely worth it in the end! You have to get a hold of your self and say, "Self, you are going to be joyful."

Your self replies, "No, I'm not going to be joyful."

And you reply even more firmly, "Oh, yes you are."

Once you take control of your inner man, your tongue will follow. If your tongue is always talking discouragement and fear—not just facing facts but talking defeatism—that is a sure barometer of what is going on inside you. It shows double-mindedness, and James 1:7-8 says that the double-minded person should not think they are going anywhere in God.

Take hold of your inner man, your thoughts, and your tongue. If you imagine yourself not making it and failing, you need to cast those thoughts down before they become a firm habit or pattern that will shipwreck your dream. Remind yourself that Jesus is the Lord of your life. He's the one who will see you through, and He's the author and finisher of your dream. If He's begun a good work in you, He's going to perform that work until you join Him in Heaven. He's working in you, on you, and through you, so you cannot allow negative thoughts to take root in your mind or to escape in your speech.

When your bucket gets kicked, what spills out? If it isn't words of faith, repent! Change your mind and get your mouth to line up with God's Word and Spirit. That is how your dream is going to become a reality in your life.

NUMBER FIVE
Mature Patience Leads to a Whole Person

The first chapter of James tells us that when patience has its perfect work, we are perfect and entire, wanting nothing. The only way we can count it joy when we fall into diverse temptations is to know that eventually we are going to be in a place of wanting nothing. That means a whole lot more than just material provision. As a matter of fact, James isn't even talking about provision there. He's talking about the reality of your faith and your walk with God. He's talking abut who you really are inside.

In order for patience to have its perfect work, you are going to have to go through a faith battle. But the victory on the other side of that battle is the new power and maturity that comes from the synergy of faith and patience. Again, synergy is when two or more things come together and become more than they would be separately. It is the potential of both elements together exploding into something neither one of them could be alone. I have used the illustration that you could pass out a thread to everyone in your church, and even the youngest and weakest could break their little thread. But if you wove the threads together and made a rope of them, no one could break the rope. That's synergy.

There is supernatural synergy with faith and patience. If you embrace this truth, you will obtain the wisdom that comes from walking with God over many years. You will follow those who through faith and patience inherited God's promises. You will refuse to be weary in well doing and reap in due season, trusting God, having His perspective, knowing your dream is going to fully manifest.

Father, we thank You for Your powerful Word. Jesus said in John 8:31-32 that if we continue in the Word, then we are true disciples, and we will know the truth, and the truth will make us free. Father, we are not only going to believe You and have faith, the substance of things we are hoping for and the evidence of things not seen, but we are going to mix patience with our faith to inherit the promise. We believe that, along with your friend Abraham, we will inherit the fulfillment of the dream You have given us. In Jesus' name we pray. Amen.

10

A FINAL OVERVIEW AND THE ULTIMATE DREAM

JOSEPH HAD A DREAM while he slept, and he awoke realizing the significance of that dream. The Holy Spirit affirmed in his heart and mind that the dream was a revelation of God's purpose and plan for his life—that he would be a great leader. He was seventeen when he had the dream, but he was thirty before it finally came to full fruition. And the thirteen years in between were some interesting years for him.

With Joseph as our primary model, we have talked about the importance of allowing God to give us a dream, which is a sense of purpose and destiny with specific goals in mind. I believe God has dreams for every one of our lives, and our inner posture regarding that belief has to be, "Father I want to dream for me what you dream for me. I want to think about me what you think about me."

God agrees! He wants us to think His thoughts about our lives and not entertain thoughts grounded in defeat, limitation, or sinful motive. He said this to His children as they were being marched into Babylonian captivity. In Jeremiah 29:11 He spoke through the prophet (my paraphrase), "You know what? You are going to have some tough times here, but I'm thinking thoughts about you that aren't like that. I'm thinking thoughts about you that are good times and not evil times, thoughts that will give you a desired end and a hope-filled, purpose-driven life."

In discussing the power and effect of having a dream, we pointed out the importance of knowing we are running a race and, just like Jesus at the Cross, we have a joy set before us that enables us to endure and see things through. Consequently, we move forward into a desired future we believe God stirred in us. And it is real. It is not just ideas or wishes or delusions of grandeur we have cooked up in our own imagination. It is our divine destiny.

Your dream has power in your life. The right dream in the right person at the right time will draw the right people into your world, and it will repel the wrong people from your life. When your dream is from God it has a life all its own within you, and it will work out in your relationships too. Let me just tell you that life is too short, and your dream is too important, to have wrong relationships in your life!

This is not to say that we judge or demean people, or (worse) that they are disposable. People are precious in God's eyes, and ultimately any dream from Him has to do with blessing and redeeming people. But the truth remains that to move on in God we need to be close to and intimate with the right people—people who will lift us up and stir us to mighty deeds.

Hebrews 10:24 says we need to be a people of God who provoke one another to love and good works, but there are some people who will just provoke us! They become a burr in our saddle, a thorn in our side, or whatever other metaphor we like to use. Nevertheless, the right dream brings the right people to us and repels the wrong people, which is a built-in blessing and defense the Lord gives us with the dream.

Our dreams will give us the wherewithal to carry on in times of difficulty, just as Joseph's dream did for him. He had a dream in the beginning, persevered in the middle, and in the end that dream came to pass. However, if we skip what happened in the middle, if we just present an abridged version, we miss a major point in the story. In those thirteen years between dream and fulfillment, it was the dream itself that kept Joseph moving forward.

Your dream will be your hope for a brighter future. Your dream has the ability to change the atmosphere in your circle of influence, whether that is your family, your workplace, your neighborhood, your nation, or even the world.

Your dream will provide proper priorities and parameters for your life. In other words, a dream from God enables you to make better decisions. If you have God's dream and are committed to it, insignificant, distracting things are much easier to spot and dismiss. Your heart and mind will say, "No, I'm not interested in that because that doesn't line up with or contribute to the dream God gave me."

Along these same lines, the increased focus the dream gives will also bring increased creativity. You'll find you have new and better ideas that come to you as you seek God and strive to fulfill the dream.

We also talked about how to know if God is giving you a dream. Although it is impossible to give a comprehensive list, one way to allow God to stir a dream in your heart is by asking the question, "What moves me to compassion?" I can promise you the devil does not motivate you by compassion, since he has no compassion in him. It is God who moves that way. If something tugs at your heart, your mind, and your emotions, and your gifts spring to life; that is a good indicator it's God. Jesus was often moved with compassion, and He was the will of God and the dream of God made flesh.

On the other hand, sometimes it is a divine frustration or discontentment that helps us understand God's dream for our lives. Moses was frustrated by the bondage of his people, so he led them into freedom. Nehemiah was frustrated by the condition of his beloved home city, Jerusalem. It had been sacked, burned, and left in ruins, so he rose up and organized people to rebuild it. Paul was frustrated by the false teachers of his day and wrote the epistles to counter them and their false doctrine. Martin Luther King Jr. was frustrated by racial inequality in America, so he said, "I have a dream," and did something about it. In many cases our frustration indicates what God has called us to do.

Sometimes you find your dream by assisting others in their dream. If you don't know what to do, find someone who does know what they want to do and partner with them. Be an Elisha. Find an Elijah and say, "I'm going to help you." Jesus said in Matthew 16:25 that in losing your life you find it. In the same way, as you help someone else who is doing something for the Lord, you often find your own dream.

A critically important thing you can do to find your life's dream is spending time in the Word of God. You must do this for yourself. Develop this discipline of a private time with God in the Word apart from other means and people. There is no replacement for the soundness of spiritual life, balance, and maturity it brings. I want to emphasize that any other means the Lord uses to develop a dream in your heart and mind must always be filtered, tested, and measured by the Word.

You might say, "Oh, but an angel came into my room in a bright light and spoke my dream with an audible voice." Okay, I'll grant that can happen to you today. God did it before, and He can do it now. But you better filter every aspect of that experience through the Word because therein is your safety net.

Likewise, while you know God can speak to you, use supernatural interventions, and employ gifts of the Spirit, you also must remember that the Bible speaks extensively about the value of wise counsel in the life of the faithful believer. This is not merely collecting opinions or getting a bunch of "yes" men and women to back you up. It has to do with transparently submitting your heart and vision to genuine, seasoned men and women of God who care about you. By listening to the Word and obtaining sound counsel from wise Christians, you have a secure foundation. Then God can use more "dramatic" means to speak to you if He desires to do so.

Your dream shows you the end from the beginning, and that knowledge grants a particular power to you. It gives you perspective when things don't seem to be going well. You also examined the emotion that accompanied the reception of the vision you received from God. Did your dream excite you or did it terrify you?

This is important because when you begin to grasp God's dream for your life, it is a natural human reaction to assess your abilities in relationship to that dream. If the result of that assessment is that you think you can do it, you will be excited. Joseph thought, "I'm going to be great leader! So, where are my followers?" He missed the mark then not so much by over- or under-estimating his abilities (it all comes from God anyway), but because he didn't understand the process God would use to develop him into that great leader he saw in his dream.

When Moses received the dream of liberating Israel from Egypt, he had already lived a lot longer than Joseph had when he received his dream. Moses had a much less naïve view of life than Joseph, but his experience still didn't give him the perspective he needed. At the end of the day, whether Moses could speak or lead or had any other natural ability didn't matter. What mattered was whether God was in it. So neither excitement ("I can do it") nor dread ("no way I can do this) are correct because what really matters is what God will do in, through, and for you.

Jesus said, "You know, if you have a little, insignificant kernel of wheat, it will never be anything more than one lonely kernel of wheat unless you bury it in the ground, cover it up, and let it die in the darkness of the soil. Only then can God breathe life into that little kernel, resurrect it, bring forth new life, and multiply it a hundred times more than the original kernel you started with" (John 12:24, my paraphrase).

That's what you have to do with your abilities. You have to lay them on the altar and say, "Father, I have got a personality, gifts, talents, abilities, and some education. I know You can use all I have, but I need You to sanctify it, energize it, bless it, and multiply it. I know that whatever it is You have called me to do, I'm insufficient for it in my own being. You and You alone are my sufficiency." Letting every part of yourself die is vital if you want God's power to flow through you and bring your dream to pass.

We also talked about the fact that your dream alone will not get you to your goal. You have to mix your dream with faith, and after you apply faith you have to mix your faith with works. Only faith followed by corresponding activity will move you forward in realizing your dream. If you aren't actively doing anything in regard to your dream, then you need to reassess where you are and what you are doing.

You must pursue your dream regardless of setbacks and circumstances. Sometimes you have time delays. Then God will move people in and out of your life that you thought might partner with you in your dream. Other times the people change because you live in a world of change. You need to know God's dream for your life isn't dependent upon any one human being's intervention.

There are often discouraging changes, and sometimes your dream morphs into something different than you originally imagined. That means the closer you get to your dream, the more you need to be prepared for it taking on a shape that looks different than you thought it would look when you started out. Nevertheless, you continue to pursue it and desire to see it through God's eyes.

Other people may try to keep you from reaching your goals, or your own limitations might hinder you. Let these things cause you to pause and strategize in order to push past the roadblock. And when looking back seems easier than moving forward, remember the Israelites. They told Moses, "We want to go back to Egypt. It was tough there, but at least we had our needs met. Out here we don't have any idea what will happen next. The Promised Land sounds great, but it's just too hard to get there. We want to go back to Egypt." When your flesh wants to dwell in the good times of your past, tell that little Israelite inside you, "Do not be weary in well doing! In due season you will reap if you don't faint."

Finally, you need to recognize the synergy of the power twins, faith and patience. Hebrews 6:12 says, **Be not slothful, but followers of them who through faith and patience inherit the promises.** The Bible instructs you to be like those believers who combine faith and patience unto the fulfillment of the promise and the inheritance that God has for you.

TRIUMPH IN DISGUISE

Although it may appear by the substance of what I have to say next that I am closing this book on a somber note, the reality is that we are taking a look at the greatest victory a Christian can experience—in disguise. I'm talking about the ultimate dream.

On Thanksgiving morning a couple of years ago my wife and I received a call from some dear members of our church, Carol and Ron. These folks had been members with us for years, and Carol had been my assistant for about twenty years. We had known their daughter Sarah, who was then a young woman, since she was a little child. They had awakened that morning, gone to Sarah's bedroom to get her up for the Thanksgiving meal, and she had gone to Heaven in her sleep. It was a great shock to them, to us, and to the entire church. We all grieved greatly.

It was during that time of grief that I started to teach a series of messages on dreams, which have become the book you are reading. Carol later told me, "You know Pastor, when you first announced you were going to be preaching for a couple months on dreams, I was devastated. It was so painful, and I was deeply upset, angry, and hurt—all those emotions that would race through a mom's mind and heart."

Carol went on to say, "I had dreams for my daughter, dreams of her getting married, having babies, of me being a grandmother to her children—all the dreams that go along with seeing the daughter you have raised stepping into full adulthood. When you said you were going to talk about dreams, I realized that those dreams for my daughter were never going to come to pass. I had to go home from church and really pray. I said, 'Lord I need your help,' and I really sought His face."

Psalm 62:8 is a beautiful verse that says, **Pour out your heart before him: God is a refuge for us.** So Carol began to pour her heart out, and the Lord spoke so beautifully to her. He said, "The ultimate dream for you, for Sarah, and for everyone, is to spend eternity in Heaven. That's the ultimate dream, and Sarah is fulfilling the ultimate dream in My presence now."

I stand by everything I have written regarding pursuing your dreams. It is sound counsel and biblical teaching, and it will help you in your life's journey. At the same time, it must be said that even if you live to be 100, in comparison to all of eternity the Bible tells us that this life is just a vapor (James 4:14). You are on Earth for a moment and then you are gone, like a blade of grass or a wildflower that fades with the summer heat. But eternity with God is forever.

Our time to make a difference in the lives of people on Earth is short and significant, but it is not the ultimate dream! We have to keep it in perspective. Then, when we have experiences that we cannot explain along the way, it is easier to cast all our cares on the Lord (1 Peter 5:7). If you don't grasp anything else, I want you to get this—don't try to explain every experience you have. Just cling to Jesus.

The human mind wants to wrap itself around everything that happens, and if you force the issue you may have to come up with your own answer. Once you start doing that, I can promise you it will be wrong. You will find yourself playing the blame game and saying things like, "It's my fault. It is all her fault. He is to blame. God didn't intervene." That's a game you will never win because the blame game is filled with anger, unforgiveness, and bitterness of soul.

When there seems to be no reason for something, I encourage you to go to the Lord like Carol did and say, "Lord, I know you are a good God. I know it is the thief who comes to steal, kill, and destroy, but You came that we might have life abundantly. Give me Your perspective on this. Help me to see this through Your eyes."

King David dealt with these issues. We have already discussed his first attempt to bring the Ark back to Jerusalem (2 Samuel 6). He threw a big party and went all out, sparing no expense—or so he thought. When the Ark had come out of Philistia years before, it had been transported on a cart. Perhaps for that reason he decided that was the right way to carry it. He made a new cart and had priests accompany it. Then, while everyone was dancing, worshipping God, and having a great time along the way, the oxen stumbled. Uzzah the priest reached out to steady the Ark, and the Bible says God struck him down dead. Talk about crashing a party!

There are some important but subtle points in this story. First, God was probably not angry at Uzzah. It is more likely that His wrath worked like gravity—automatically. If you break His laws (natural or spiritual) there are immediate consequences, and touching the Ark was not allowed in the Old Covenant. With no redemption through the Cross yet available, Uzzah inadvertently broke God's law and died.

Second, we need to understand David's emotions. He called that place "Perez-uzzah," which means "break of Uzzah."[3] It appears on the surface that he probably was blaming Uzzah, but the Hebrew words describing David's emotions in 2 Samuel 6:8-9 were anger and a holy fear of God.[4]

---

[3] James Strong, *Exhaustive Concordance of the Bible*, "Hebrew and Chaldee Dictionary," (Nashville, TN: Thomas Nelson Publishers, 1984), #6560.

[4] James Strong, *Exhaustive Concordance of the Bible*, "Hebrew and Chaldee Dictionary," #2734, #3372.

Put yourself in David's place. He was throwing God a big party, his heart was right, he was doing God's will, and God struck one of the party's organizers dead, stopping the parade in its tracks. The truth is, David and the priests knew the Law. They knew the Ark was to be carried only on poles by the priests. They knew it was not to be transported on a cart or touched by human hands. But when their error cost them Uzzah's life, David was devastated. He was furious with himself for being so cavalier about God's Law, and his fear of and reverence for God's Word overwhelmed him.

This experience shut down David's drive to return the Ark. He literally said, **How shall the ark of the Lord come to me? "** (2 Samuel 6:9). That's when he diverted the Ark to the home of Obed-Edom because he was afraid of being too close to God. Of course, God blessed Odem-Edom, and after stewing in his anger, grief, and guilt for awhile, David reached the point where he missed the presence of the Lord more than He feared Him. He realized he had missed great blessing for all those months because he had kept God at arm's length. That's when he brought the Ark home—and this time he did it right.

This story of David illustrates human error causing tragedy. Imperfect human beings mess up, but God is always good and faithful to His Word. Knowing this, there are still times when things happen and God doesn't tell us why, like when Sarah went to Heaven. For everyone who knew her, there was no reason for her early departure. All we know is that this is a fallen, sinful, imperfect world, where suffering and difficulty are part of the picture. And sometimes people go to Heaven too soon for us.

If life went perfectly and answers were clear, Jesus wouldn't need to come back and rule in person. But we see through a glass darkly (1 Corinthians 13:12). And when He comes back or we get to Heaven, we won't care about many of the whys and wherefores, but we will have the answers to all our questions.

If you have had a life experience you can't explain, rest in God. Stay close to Him. And live by faith. If someone tries to come up with an explanation for something in your life or you are tempted to do so for someone else, just hold your peace, be a blessing, and move on. Above all, don't let your lack of understanding drive you away from the Lord or kill your dream!

David learned that lesson during his experience with the Ark. We know because in 2 Samuel 12:16-23 he dealt with a child who was very sick. He fasted and prayed, but the child still died. When that happened, he washed, dressed in fine clothes, and came out looking totally at peace. His servants were shocked and asked him why he was not overcome with grief. David said to them, **While the child was yet alive, I fasted and wept: for I said, Who** can tell whether God will be gracious to me, that the child may live? But now he is dead, wherefore should I fast? can I bring him back again? I shall go to him, but he shall not return to me. David understood the ultimate dream.

I firmly believe if Sarah had the opportunity to come back today, she would decline. I believe once you have experienced Heaven there is no way you are coming back! We have all lost loved ones, family members and spiritual brothers and sisters who influenced us in an important way, people who were pillars in our lives and brought us tremendous blessing. They have gone on, and we can't bring them back. But like David said, we will go to them! That is our great hope and ultimate dream in Jesus.

Colossians 3:1-2 says, **If ye then be risen with Christ, seek those things which are above, where Christ sitteth on the right hand of God. Set your affection on things above, not on things on the earth.** While we appreciate God's blessings here on Earth, and we know He wants our dreams from Him to propel us and count for something in this life, the final reality is that everything we do here is for Heaven. The more we focus upon the eternal things, and the more we see our dreams as taking as many people to Heaven with us as possible, the healthier we will be spiritually.

I love and appreciate T. L. Osborn. He is a great apostle who has been to the four corners of this Earth. There was a time when he had preached to more people in person than any other human being. Someone may have surpassed that by now, but it is a tremendous testimony of a ministry greatly used by God.

T. L. always ties everything to the eternal. On one occasion I was a day speaker at a conference, and he was a night speaker. During a break he talked to some of us young ministers about money. He has always been one of the must frugal ministers I know, and he said, "Let me tell you something, Preacher. If you are going to be successful in ministry, you have to know how to get the money. I believe God for the money because it is going to take money to do what God has called me to do. And the money you spend on your own tranquility is the best money you will ever spend. Don't get so busy that you forget to hear from God. Learn to create an atmosphere of tranquility, for in that atmosphere God can give you ideas, and one idea can be worth a million souls."

There it was again. He was thinking in terms of eternal souls, putting money in the context of eternity. He was saying we can live in a nice house, but having a nice house is just to provide an atmosphere in which we can rest in God, hear from Him, and get ideas that will win people to the Lord Jesus Christ.

In all you do and aim for, set your affection on eternal things not on temporary things. Turn your heart and mind toward things that are above and not on things of this Earth. You want to be blessed and God wants to bless you. You want to receive His dream for your life and fulfill it while you are here on Earth. But you must always measure what you desire by eternal significance.

Hebrews 11 lists the great men and women of faith, the saints of old. The Holy Spirit reveals the significance of their lives along with their dreams and how each ran their race and completed it—even though some died before seeing their dream come to pass. Hebrews 12:1-2 continues, **Wherefore seeing we also are compassed about with so great a cloud of witnesses, let us lay aside every weight, and the sin which doth so easily beset us, and let us run with patience the race that is set before us, Looking unto Jesus the author and finisher of our faith.**

Jesus is the author of our dream, and He will be the finisher of our dream. If He started us, He will finish us. Verse 2 goes on to say, **who for the joy that was set before him endured the cross, despising the shame, and is set down at the right hand of the throne of God.** Even Jesus had a dream, and that dream is expressed with the words **the joy that was set before Him.**

Jesus had a dream that enabled Him to endure the Cross, and verse 3 says, **For consider him that endured such contradiction of sinners against himself, lest ye be wearied and faint in your minds.** Pursuing your dream is not always going to be rosy, easy, or a walk in the park.

That's when you need to consider Jesus because the beautiful part is, Jesus' dream was fulfilled, and because His dream was fulfilled your dream can be fulfilled. Because He lives you live. Even if fulfillment comes down to the eternal state, Heaven itself, Jesus is the Lord of all dreams, all dreamers, and all fulfillments. That is the ultimate dream.

Carol won her inner battle over the loss of her daughter and the difficulty she initially had about my series of messages on dreams. God gave her joy, and she sent me a note that said, "The Lord has spoken to my heart, and I am at peace—the ultimate dream. So preach your series and write your book, because I have a grasp of God's ultimate dream for me."

As I said earlier, every month I take people to visit Oral Roberts. This blesses him because he can't get out to preach anymore and he can to preach to us. It's always wonderful, and we share with him how his ministry has influenced and blessed and enriched our lives. We always have a question or two, and he will usually take five or ten minutes to answer. Then he lays hands on us, occasionally giving a word to some, and it is just a great time.

While Oral's wife Evelyn was still living I took a group, and before we left Oral asked us to pray for them. We encircled Oral and Evelyn, and she said, "Now I want you all to pray that we'll go to Heaven soon."

That was tough for me! Oral has been a mentor and a spiritual father to me, and he's been with me though all sorts of milestones. When Melissa and I were having trouble conceiving, he prayed and soon she was pregnant. When we needed to buy our first home and didn't have any money, he prayed and prophesied, and soon we had our first home. When we got ready to buy land for the church, Oral walked the property with me, we prayed, and God gave us the land. So he has been an integral part of our lives, and I am in no hurry for him to go home!

But there was Evelyn, all cheery, saying, "Pray that we'll go to Heaven soon."

Mike Maiden, our friend from Phoenix, was there and prayed, "Lord, give Evelyn and Oral the desire of their hearts. If they want to go home, take them home." A few weeks later Evelyn had gone to Heaven.

After Evelyn had gone to Heaven, I was with Oral and it was time for him to pray for me. He has a little stool that you sit on, and he lays his hands on you. I was on the stool, he was in his chair, and he leaned over and put his hands on me, saying, "You can count on me Jeff. I'll be cheering you on from Heaven."

When I realized he was talking about himself and his own departure, I opened my eyes and said, "Don't be in a hurry." But at almost ninety years old, Heaven is so real to him. He sees himself there, standing with Evelyn and cheering me on.

When eternal realities begin to overshadow the things of this life, then you know you have taken hold of the ultimate dream. And when you lose yourself in the ultimate dream, it is so much easier to walk out the dream God has given you for your life on Earth now. You can be like Jesus, enduring all the trials and challenges—and the pain and the sorrows—with joy. You won't give in to self-pity or anger or bitterness because you have your feet firmly planted in eternity. You know where you are headed in *Making Your Dreams a Reality!*

ABOUT THE AUTHOR

JEFF WALKER was born and raised in the State of Illinois. He attended Central Bible College of the Assemblies of God and is a graduate of Rhema Bible Training Center. He earned a Bachelor of Arts degree from Western Illinois University, Bachelor of Science in Psychology and Master of Arts in Professional Counseling degrees from Liberty University, Master of Divinity and Doctor of Ministry degrees from Oral Roberts University, and a Doctor of Clinical Psychology degree from Trinity College of Graduate Studies, which included an internship at the Betty Ford Center.

Dr. Walker holds ecclesiastical credentials with the Rhema Ministerial Association International. He serves on the Board of Trustees of Oral Roberts' Charismatic Bible Ministries organization, the Board of Directors of Dwight Thompson Ministries, the Board of Regents of Bethel Christian College, and the Board of Directors of Victory Christian Center.

Dr. Walker has been a reserve deputy sheriff and departmental chaplain for the Riverside County Sheriff's Department since 1990. He also served as a member of the Desert Regional Mental Health Advisory Board from 1994 to 1995. In 2008 he presented a psycho-educational seminar for pastors entitled, "Knowing When and How to Refer a Congregant to a Mental Health Professional," at the Christian Association for Psychological Studies (CAPS) world conference. And he assists individuals with chronic severe mental illness at an outpatient county mental health clinic two days a week.

Having received a call to ministry at eighteen years of age, Dr. Walker served two congregations as associate pastor. He then felt led of the Lord in February of 1982 to start Victory Christian Center in Palm Springs, California. In 1985 the congregation acquired eleven acres located on Bob Hope Drive in Rancho Mirage, California. The Victory campus is home to the church as well as Victory Christian School, Southern California Christian College, and the church offices.

Dr. Walker, who has ministered extensively throughout the U.S. and abroad, resides in Rancho Mirage, California, with his wife Melissa and their children, Rebekah, Amen, and Caleb.

TO CONTACT THE AUTHOR:
P.O. Box 5060 Palm Springs, CA 92263
www.DrJeffWalker.com
760.328.3313

THE CROSS STAFF was developed by the medieval Jewish scholar Levi ben Gersohn around 1342. It was used by most of the early explorers, including guiding Columbus to the New World and the Pilgrims on the Mayflower to religious freedom. It seems unlikely that any of these early pioneers missed the symbolism of this navigational tool—finding their course in life by looking at the world through the cross.

We at CrossStaff Publishing believe that it is through the Cross that life's answers are found. Just as ancient mariners had little room for excess baggage, we feel that readers should benefit from materials that reach right into the heart and deal with life's core issues. The purpose of all our materials is to equip you, the reader, to more accurately align your life with the Cross. For without the Cross, we are adrift and without the proper orientation to navigate life's storms and uncharted waters.

Additional copies of this book are available at your local bookstore.

Additional copies of this book
are available at your local bookstore.

CrossStaff Publishing, LLC
P.O. Box 288
Broken Arrow, Oklahoma 74013-0288
www.CrossStaff.com

CROSSSTAFF
PUBLISHERS, LLC